TELESHOCK

How to Survive the Break-up of Ma Bell

TELESHOCK

How to Survive the Break-up of Ma Bell

William J. Cook
and
Christopher Ma

A WALLABY BOOK

PUBLISHED BY POCKET BOOKS NEW YORK

Another *Original* publication of Wallaby Books

A Wallaby Book published by
POCKET BOOKS, a division of Simon & Schuster, Inc.
1230 Avenue of the Americas, New York, N.Y. 10020

Copyright © 1985 by William J. Cook and Christopher Ma
Cover artwork copyright © 1985 by Magic Image Studio, Ltd.

ISBN: 0-671-55400-X

First Wallaby Books printing July, 1985

10 9 8 7 6 5 4 3 2 1

WALLABY and colophon are registered trademarks
of Simon & Schuster, Inc.

Printed in the U.S.A.

ACKNOWLEDGMENTS

For several years we have both been observing and writing about the changing world of telephony from our posts in the Washington bureau of *Newsweek*. Shortly after the Bell System officially was broken up, one of us had a dream—or maybe it was a nightmare—in which a dentist methodically pulled each of his teeth and replaced it with a telephone. It seemed a sure sign that we should write a practical guide to the enormous and confusing changes taking place in the American phone system.

Many members of the telephone industry helped us with this book, and the fact that we are not able to mention each of them here in no way reflects on the appreciation we have for their contributions. We would be remiss in not acknowledging the special assistance of at least a few of our sources, however. Pic Wagner, AT&T's Washington spokesman; Gary Tobin, who speaks for MCI; and Chris Valmassei and Roberta Weiner of Bell Communications Research were not only invaluable in arranging interviews for us, but provided many useful ideas.

Others whose help we could not have done without include Linda Haase of Allnet Communications Services; Robert Focazio and Rudy Marzano of AT&T Information Systems; Patty Wainwright of AT&T Communications; Robert Valentini of Bell Atlantic; Web Chamberlin and Richard Ellis of Chesapeake & Potomac Telephone Company; Carol Crawford, William De-Kay, and Read Clarke of GTE Sprint; James Ferguson, Robert Swezey, and Barry Thomas of MCI; and Fritz Witti of Satellite Business Systems. We are also grateful to Sam Simon of the Telecommunications Research & Action Center and Robert Krughoff of the Center for the Study of Services, publisher of the excellent Consumers' CHECKBOOK guide to lower phone costs in 1984.

Larry Povich, Ellen Rafferty and Michael Deuel Sullivan at the Federal Communications Commission helped us with several important problems. Ann Director of Telocator Network of America and Stuart Crump, Jr., publisher of *Personal Communications,* explained some of the mysteries of pagers and cellular telephones to us. Other valuable assistance came from Arthur Latno of Pacific Telesis and Michael Perlman, telecommunications consultant in the Washington office of Touche Ross. We also thank Harry Newton, publisher of *Teleconnect* magazine, an indispensable and entertaining guide to the telephone industry. A number of the above were kind enough to review portions of the manuscript for us, although it goes without saying that any mistakes made are ours, not theirs.

We especially wish to thank our research associate Arthur R. Brodsky, who contributed heavily to the chapters on answering machines, 800 and 900 numbers, the revolution in long distance service, and on how to handle telephone harassment and emergencies. Brodsky's editorial assistance was of enormous help throughout the project.

Our *Newsweek* colleague Ib Ohlsson drew the illustrations for our chapters on wiring and repair. He was, as always, the consummate professional. We also thank Mel Elfin of *Newsweek* for his encouragement during the writing of this book, and Sydny Miner, our editor at Pocket Books, for keeping the project speeding along.

Above and beyond all else, we wish to thank Ann Z. Cook and Nathalie Gilfoyle, whose editing skills were only exceeded by their patience in managing the chaos of the lives we shared with them while this book was being written. The book would not exist without them.

William J. Cook
Christopher Ma

Washington, DC
January 1985

AUTHORS' NOTE

As we state throughout the book, practically everything about telephones is changing very rapidly. That is especially true of prices and services. The prices and services we have quoted were valid in January 1985.

CONTENTS

TELESHOCK

How to Survive the Break-up of Ma Bell

CHAPTER 1 Surviving the Break-up of Ma Bell

Practically everyone we know is confused, even angry, by what has happened to the telephone. That familiar service used to be brought to you by one of the most boringly dependable institutions on earth, the American Telephone & Telegraph Company—Ma Bell and her many children. The phone worked when you picked up the receiver. Your relatives on the far side of the country sounded as clear on the phone as someone across town. When you had a problem, which was almost never, a smiling repair person in a shiny truck with the bell on the side quickly appeared. He or she didn't charge.

Today everything appears to have changed, for AT&T, *the telephone company*, has been broken up. Now the consumer who once got everything from a single entity is faced with buying or leasing phones from one company, placing local calls with a second, relying on one or more additional companies for long-distance service, and requiring the assistance of still others, should the phones need repair. While long-distance rates fell more than 6 percent the first year after the phone company was broken up, local rates went up more than that, worrying and angering phone customers.

It used to be that you never had to think about your telephone. It was just there, and you used it as necessary. Now you have a lot more choices, and a lot more responsibilities, and a lot more frustrations, than ever in the past.

• You must decide whether to buy your phones or continue to rent them from AT&T. If you buy, how do you choose from among the hundreds of phones for sale at department stores, hardware stores, phone stores, even auto parts stores?

• You must decide which long-distance company will serve as your primary carrier. How do you decide among companies offering everything from cheap rates to American Tourister luggage?

• You must arrange for repairs on your telephone yourself, even if you still rent it. Who can fix your phone?

• You now own the telephone wires inside your residence. If you want to change the location of your phone, how do you do it? Can you do it yourself?

• You now get a telephone bill that is several pages long. How do you read it? Are you taking the local service option that is best and cheapest for you?

• You can buy all kinds of new telephone equipment, including answering machines, cordless telephones, and cellular radio-telephones. You can even hook your personal computer to the telephone. But is it worth doing?

These are not trivial questions. Enormous sums of money are involved. There are 133 million residential telephones and 48 million business telephones in the United States today. In 1985, for example, 28 million telephones worth nearly $1 billion are expected to be sold in the United States. Those are regular phones, the ones with cords. There will be an additional 6.5 million cordless phones valued at $500 million, and 3.5 million answering machines worth $290 million sold to American consumers. Together these consumers make over 250 billion telephone calls a year. You need only to watch Joan Rivers and Cliff Robertson hawk long-distance services on television to understand that the telephone companies know they are playing for big stakes, an estimated $48 billion long-distance market in 1985.

What happened to the telephone company, anyway? AT&T, the world's largest company, had a monopoly on local telephone service over 80 percent of the United States. In exchange for being the sole provider of telephone service, the parent company and its subsidiaries were regulated by state authorities and the Federal Communications Commission. But the government's antitrust lawyers always feared that with its enormous power AT&T could "reach out and crush someone."

The federal government brought antitrust suits against AT&T twice. After the first suit, brought in 1949, AT&T agreed in 1956 to confine its activities to communications, in exchange for being allowed to keep its huge Western Electric manufacturing subsidiary. That meant, for practical purposes, that AT&T could not compete in the new computer industry. Technology was beginning to close in on its monopoly.

The Justice Department filed a second antitrust suit in 1974, charging the company with keeping potential competitors out of equipment and long-distance markets. This time the Justice Department was not alone. There was also a barrage of private antitrust suits brought by other companies—including its present long-distance competitor, MCI—claiming that AT&T would not let them compete. All the while, the FCC had been chipping away at AT&T's monopoly, ruling in 1968 that non-Bell equipment could be attached to the telephone, in 1969 that MCI could build a microwave long-distance system to compete with AT&T in certain markets, and in 1977 that you could own your own telephones.

The government's antitrust case against AT&T was strong, and U.S. District Court Judge Harold H. Greene, who was trying the case, wrote rulings during the trial that suggested he would rule against the company. As MCI Chairman William McGowan said gleefully, "They were erecting the scaffolding outside the courtroom." Against this ominous backdrop, AT&T and the Justice Department got together during the trial and worked out an agreement. It was announced at noon on a historic Friday in January 1982. AT&T Chairman Charles L. Brown's eyes became misty and his voice husky as he described the terms of the agreement. AT&T agreed to give up its twenty-two operating companies, the providers of local telephone service, on New Year's Day 1984, in exchange for the ability to compete in markets that had been closed to the company under the 1956 settlement.

ABC television's David Brinkley expressed the sentiments of many when he scoffed that the Justice Department had jeopardized "one of the few services in this country that still works." He suggested that the government lawyers "ought to be made to wear cowbells around their necks" so that citizens can always know where they are and what they are up to. Nearly a year after divestiture became effective, a *Business Week*/Harris Poll found that by a margin of 64 percent to 25 percent, Americans agreed the breakup was a bad idea.

AT&T was broken up for antitrust reasons, to be sure, but technology, not the law, was the real driving force. Bell Laboratories had developed key building blocks of the new technologies, including the transistor, but under the law, AT&T could not participate in the computer revolution. The growth of computers and electronic transmission of data meant that telephone systems and computing systems were converging technically, as computers needed to communicate and communications systems needed to compute. A senior telephone executive explained that "over the past two decades, many forces were at work to change the way in which telephone service is provided. The most evident was the political move toward competition, but underlying it was the technology explosion that made the introduction of competition possible, and perhaps inevitable."

AT&T, now a smaller company (though still one of the largest in the country), has two major parts: AT&T Communications, the long-distance company, and AT&T Technologies, which includes the famed Bell Laboratories, the former Western Electric, and AT&T Information Systems, the company's marketing arm, as well as AT&T International, which has plunged into foreign markets from which the company withdrew in 1925. Ma Bell's former children, the twenty-two Bell operating companies, were formed into seven regional companies: NYNEX, BellSouth, Ameritech, Pacific Telesis, Southwestern Bell, US West, and Bell Atlantic. Local telephone service continues to be a regulated monopoly.

If imitation is the sincerest form of flattery, the Japanese would appear to agree with the breakup of AT&T. Nippon Telegraph & Telephone Public Corporation, Japan's monopoly phone company, will be broken up in 1985, along lines similar to the AT&T divestiture. The NTT breakup won't be the result of court action, however. It will come after long consultation between the government, NTT, and the communications industry, with all three agreeing that long-distance and new communications services thrive best in a competitive environment.

With the breakup of their giant telephone companies, the United States and Japan are positioning themselves for leadership in the Information Age. The two nations are creating a yeasty competitive environment for new information services to flourish. AT&T's Charles L. Brown says that "no longer is a telephone simply an instrument for voice communications, but rather an information terminal, a means of accessing and exchanging information in a variety of ways, to and from a variety of sources." Arno Penzias, a Nobel laureate and Bell Laboratories' vice-president for research, says, "we've done the job for voice. Now we need to do the job for people's machines."

Your telephone—or your telephone line—is your personal plug into the Information Age. Already, as we describe in the following pages, you can dial up computer data bases around the world, from home. You can bank at home. You can turn your furnace on and off by calling it on the telephone. If you are elderly or infirm and can't get to your telephone, you can push a button on a little transmitter that hangs around your neck to make your telephone call for help.

All these wonders are a far cry from "Plain Old Telephone Service"—and P.O.T.S. is going to be difficult enough for the next few years till everyone gets used to the new telephone system. In the long run, the breakup of Ma Bell may mean better telephone service at lower prices for most consumers. On the other hand, as the economist John Maynard Keynes once observed, "In the long run we are all dead."

In the meantime, we hope you'll find that our little book will ease your telephone frustrations, introduce you to some exciting new telephone technologies, and help you to save money. We'd like to think you'll use our book the way parents use Dr. Benjamin Spock's classic, *Baby and Child Care*. Whenever you have a telephone question, grab for *Teleshock*.

We start with your telephone, whether to buy it or lease it, and what to look for, should you decide to buy. You're now responsible for your own telephone installation and repair, and we explain in simple terms how to install a phone, how to add an extension, and what to do when your phone breaks. Our essential message here is that you really can do it yourself.

Nearly all of us are going to have to decide between now and the end of 1986 which long-distance company will be our primary carrier. We show you how to look beyond the television ads in making your decision. We give you the tools to decide which local service option to select for yourself, explain how to read your phone bill to make sure that's what you are getting, and show you how to complain if you're not.

Then we describe the realm of telephony beyond P.O.T.S., the new world of sophisticated answering machines, cordless telephones, and super-high-quality cellular telephones for your car or briefcase. We show how you can buy an inexpensive pager to clip on your child so you can "beep" him or her when it's time to come home. We summarize the exciting new services—and lifestyles—that are available once you hook a personal computer to the telephone.

Small business has been dealt a particularly lousy hand by telephone divestiture. While a residential phone user may be frustrated, a small business that spends a lot on telephones and telephone services, as most do, can be hurt badly by a wrong telephone decision. We devote an extensive section to small business telephone survival, including the phones and services that are available and how to buy them.

Finally, we look at FuturePhone, at the array of telephone wonders that's just ahead. You may have your own personal telephone number that follows you around. You'll be able to play games on the phone. You'll even be able to tell who is calling you before you pick up the phone. Telephony will become, as someone has observed, one step short of telepathy.

SECTION

1

Your Telephone

CHAPTER 2 Should You Lease or Buy Your Phone?

If you didn't know that you can now own your own phones rather than lease them from AT&T, you're hardly alone. Despite the fact that the Federal Communications Commission has allowed customer-owned equipment in the home since 1977, many consumers still don't realize that they can now be owners rather than renters of their telephones.

Why bother? you ask. The old system seemed to work pretty well. That's true, of course. But if you do a little back-of-the-envelope figuring, you'll see that the old way was (and is) surprisingly expensive when compared to buying your own equipment. Assume, for instance, that you're part of the 80 percent of all U.S. households that received local telephone service from the Bell System before divestiture. Under an option that will be available to you until at least January 1, 1986, AT&T will sell to you for $19.95 any traditional rotary-style phone that you had been leasing from one of its former local operating company subsidiaries, such as New York Telephone, before divestiture. AT&T's rental rate for such a phone would be $1.50 per month. By dividing the cost of purchasing your plain old rotary-dial phone by the monthly expense of renting

The White House says to stand by... The President hasn't decided whether to buy or lease the phone—

HOT LINE

Reprinted by permission: Tribune Media Services, Inc.

the instrument from AT&T instead, you'd see that you would pay for your investment within fourteen months.

While the break-even point for buying the same type of phone new doesn't come quite as soon, the economic case for buying, rather than renting, is still strong. According to a study by the Center for the Study of Services, a leading Washington, D.C.-based consumer organization, your break-even point for buying, rather than renting, a basic rotary-dial phone new at an AT&T Phone Center would be about twenty-one months. That pay-back period could be cut to as little as seventeen months if you did your shopping at one of the many retail stores that are competing aggressively with AT&T on price.

While you'll find that both leasing costs and purchase prices will vary depending on the kind of phone you have or want at home, the methodology for determining the point at which you'll save by buying, rather than renting, your own instruments will always be the same. Just *divide purchase price by monthly rental charges* to calculate how many months you would have to lease your phone to cover the cost of buying one yourself. Since a good quality phone will generally work well for at least ten years, you'll see that the financial benefits of buying your own telephones can be impressive.

For those of you who are currently renting phones from AT&T the following table will show exactly where your break-even point falls in buying, rather than leasing, your present equipment.

TABLE 1
Telephone Purchase Break-even Points

Telephone Type	AT&T Monthly Rental Rates To January 1, 1986	AT&T Purchase Prices for Phones Currently Leased	Break-Even Point
Traditional Desktop (Rotary)	$1.50	$19.95	14 mon.
Traditional Wall (Rotary)	$1.50	$19.95	14 mon.
Traditional Desktop (Touch-tone)	$2.85	$41.95	15 mon.
Traditional Wall (Touch-tone)	$2.85	$41.95	15 mon.
Princess (Rotary)	$3.15	$39.94	13 mon.
Princess (Touch-tone)	$4.05	$49.95	13 mon.
Trimline Desktop (Rotary)	$3.45	$44.95	14 mon.
Trimline Wall (Rotary)	$3.45	$44.95	14 mon.
Trimline Desktop (Touch-tone)	$4.60	$54.95	12 mon.
Trimline Wall (Touch-tone)	$4.60	$54.95	12 mon.

Because new phones vary widely in price, depending on whose equipment you're buying and where you're buying it, it's impossible to identify precisely where you'll break even in the purchase of various types of new instruments. But the Center for the Study of Services suggests that the payback period will average only twelve months for a new Trimline tone wall phone to seventeen months for a new, standard rotary-dial desk model. If you buy your Trimline Desktop touch-tone phone for $54.95 and keep it for ten years, you'll save $497.05.

Despite the economic advantages of buying rather than renting, some of you may still prefer to lease your equipment. Renting always requires less cash outlay up front. If you're pinched for cash and don't want to use a credit card, then renting your phone is the obvious alternative.

Just as there are consumers who would rather buy a quart of milk at the corner store than drive to the supermarket for a better price, many of you may be willing to pay a premium for the convenience of not having to shop for a telephone. But don't make the mistake of thinking that if you continue to pay for your phones the old-fashioned way, which is to rent them, you'll get good, old-fashioned telephone company service if your phone breaks. While the company that rents you the telephone—since divestiture, that's AT&T, not the local operating companies—is still responsible for fixing your equipment, the day when the phone company would send a serviceperson out to your house for free has gone the way of milk and bread delivery men. For a telephone repairperson to visit you today will cost at least $25, and probably more. We outline in Chapter 7 what you have to do to get a telephone fixed. But for now, just keep in mind that when it comes to telephone repair and maintenance, the advantages of leasing over owning aren't nearly what they used to be.

AT&T's Deal That They Hope You Can't Refuse

Do you agree that buying makes more sense than renting, but dread the hassles that come with shopping? The easiest way to buy a phone, bar none, is to purchase the instrument you already have at home from AT&T. Heretical as it may sound, we have friends working for competitors of AT&T who chose to buy the AT&T phones they had at home, rather than spend the time to hunt elsewhere.

To make the purchase, all you have to do is call AT&T toll-free at 1-800-555-8111, twenty-four hours a day, seven days a week, and tell the sales representative which of your phones you wish to buy. You'll find the applicable prices in Table 1. You can pay by check if you like, or you can charge your purchases to VISA, MasterCard or American Express. In most states AT&T will also allow you to pay in interest-free installments billed to you through one of its former offspring, your local telephone operating company.

When you buy phones already in your home, the warranty on the equipment is ninety days. Because of the quality of AT&T's phones, it's unlikely that you'll need to invoke the warranty. But if you have even the slightest doubts about your present equipment, there's a way to buy yourself additional insurance. Before you buy, return the phones you rent to AT&T and ask for replacements on a rental basis. Sometimes the replacements will be totally new equipment. At other times they'll be telephones that were used by other customers but refurbished at an AT&T factory so that they're as good as new. Whatever the case, there doesn't have to be anything wrong with your equipment to demand an exchange. Preferring another color or thinking the phone looks dirty are reasons enough to request a trade. Once you've had your new equipment on a rental basis for even a day or two, you can buy it from AT&T at the same price that would have applied to the old telephones. (On a standard rotary-dial phone, the difference between AT&T's new and used phone prices is almost $20.) Any monthly rental charges that you've been paying for your phones will stop on the day AT&T processes your purchase order.

For pure convenience, AT&T's program for selling you your current phones is hard to beat. Price and warranty-wise, there's room for improvement, however. While you can buy the traditional desk model touch-tone phone in your home from AT&T for $41.95 and get a ninety-day warranty, some of AT&T's competitors offer an equivalent brand-new phone for about the same price, and provide warranties that are often as long as one or two years.

Price Is a Priority, but Not the Only One

We don't know who first said, "If the wagon ain't broke, don't fix it," but it's an adage that frustrated consumers frequently invoke these days in denouncing the government and the court's decision to deregulate the telephone business. We're not just being Pollyannas, we hope, in suggesting that by opening up the industry to competition, there have been at least a few benefits to the calling public. Prominent among them is the tremendous proliferation in retail stores selling phones today, and the lower equipment prices that such competition brings.

Just look around the next time you go to the drugstore, super-market, lumberyard, or hardware store. In the brave new world after Ma Bell, everyone is selling telephones. Trying to pick among the many vendors can be as risky as buying a used car. There are almost as many variations on prices, features, warranties, and service arrangements as there are tea leaves in China. As a smart consumer, you'll want the phones you buy to be well-built, fit your needs, and be competitively priced. But don't get too compulsive about your shopping. Life is too short to treat phone buying as if it were the search for the Holy Grail.

We don't know the best store in your city to buy phones, but you'll find some guidance on prices in a shopping survey that's been done by the Center for the Study of Services. According to the Center's research, catalogue showrooms are usually the cheapest places to buy telephones, followed by discount appliance and discount department stores, drugstores, hardware and lumber stores. The most expensive vendors are often full-service department stores, telephone specialty stores, and electronics boutiques.

Besides these outlets, you can still go to either AT&T or your local telephone operating company to buy new phones. The equipment you will get from them will be top of the line in quality, but also near the top of the line in price. If you're buying from your local phone company out of a desire to stick with name brands, you should know that many of the phones sold by such local operating companies as New York and New England Tel are now made by manufacturers other than AT&T. While the quality is likely to be the same, the parentage won't be.

Don't Underestimate the Importance of Warranties and Service

Not long ago one of our journalistic colleagues accidentally dropped the basic touch-tone desk phone in his office and had to call in a local telephone company repairman to administer first aid. On the inside cover of the phone, when the telephone company man took it apart, was another repairman's note that the phone had last been serviced in 1969. It was wonderful testament to the quality of the phones AT&T used to make at its Western Electric subsidiary.

AT&T still makes phones that are "built to last," and so do several other manufacturers, among them ITT, GTE, and Comdial. But as a senior AT&T executive once admitted to us, even AT&T will probably never make phones as durable as the plain old telephones that Western Electric used to make.

What all this means is that the kind of warranty and return policies, and maintenance and service commitments that accompany your purchase of a new phone, are important considerations. A phone that sounds fine in the store can go on the blink within hours or days of coming home with you. This is especially true of some of the newer electronic phones, which frequently have more features than their traditional electromechanical counterparts, and thus can break more easily. Cordless phones require an even stronger caution because the radio frequencies on which they operate in your home may carry static that was never a problem in the store. (For more on cordless phones, see Chapter 14.)

To protect yourself against a lemon, be sure that the store where you buy your phone gives you at least a week to return it. If the store where you're shopping only allows store credits or merchandise exchanges for returned products, make certain you patronize that store often enough to put such credits to good use.

During the exchange period, use the new phone as often as possible to try to find any bugs that it might have. You might discover, for instance, that a phone sounds fine in the store where there's no one listening in on an extension line, but is too weak to make your voice heard properly when there are others joining in from extension lines around the house. That's because telephones all require a little electrical current to work, and when there are too many extension phones demanding juice from the line at the same time, none can get enough to perform correctly.

Once you've passed the exchange period, you'll have to look to the manufacturer's warranty to repair or replace your new equipment, should it develop problems. A number of telephone makers, including AT&T, ITT, and GTE, provide a one-year warranty on new phones. Comdial, which is a leading independent telephone manufacturer, offers its customers a two-year warranty. If your phone breaks during the warranty period, that usually entitles you to ask the manufacturer to repair or replace the equipment at no charge to you. Sometimes the store where you bought the phone will send the defective instrument back to the manufacturer for you. At other times you'll have to arrange for the shipping yourself. For details on how to have a phone repaired, see Chapter 7.

In a few cases, retailers may offer their own warranties (some at a charge, some for free) and have their own repair shops on the premises. That eliminates the hassle of having to ship your phone back to the manufacturer and can cut down on the time necessary to fix your problem. Sometimes stores that repair phones on the premises will lend you a phone while they're repairing yours. Don't be bashful about asking for a loaner.

A $10 Phone Is a $10 Phone, or, Some Further Do's and Don't's on Purchasing a Telephone

Consider what you'll be doing with the phone before writing your check. If all you need is an extension phone to keep by your basement workbench, then one of those one-piece phones, cheap enough to throw away if it breaks, may be all you require. But if you're shopping for a phone that will be used more frequently, you're probably smart to invest a little more.

It's a bit of a saw, we know, but as with most things, when it comes to buying a telephone, you get what you pay for. A $10 disposable phone made in Hong Kong works a lot better than having to string tin cans across your neighbor's fence, but we've yet to find a disposable phone that didn't sound tinny. You'd be surprised how quickly a phone like this can drive you crazy.

Expect, as a general rule, to have to spend at least $35 for a rotary-dial phone with good sound quality. If you're looking for a touch-tone phone, you'll have to pay $50 to $60 for even a stripped-down model. Don't expect these thresholds to come down anytime soon. While you may find phone makers including more features at these price levels in a year or two, they're not eager to see the prices on quality phones fall much below their current levels. At less than $30, a good-quality phone isn't likely to have a big enough profit margin for retailers to want to carry the product on their shelves.

For a consumer, there's no substitute, of course, for getting out and kicking the tires before making your buying decision. We've included in Table 2 a list of things you'll want to check. Pick up the receiver and test the way it feels, for instance. Be sure the mouthpiece and earpiece are positioned properly, so that you don't find yourself talking into outer space or cricking your neck in order to hear.

Now look at the dial or keypad. Does everything work? Can you read the numbers clearly? Have letters been included with the numerals so that you'll know how to dial the BUtterfield-8 exchange when a member of the Anti-Digit Dialing League* gives you his number?

If the store where you are shopping permits, plug the phone in and place a call. Listen to how the person you called sounds on the line, and ask that person how well you sound. Then request that the party call you back so that you can hear the ring. Otherwise you may find yourself following in the footsteps of a friend of ours. After spending a full morning calling his friends from the telephone

---

TABLE 2
A Buyer's Checklist

Ask Yourself	Yes	No
1. Is the phone comfortable to hold?		
2. Can you work the dial or keypad easily?		
3. Are you getting a touch-tone phone if needed?		
4. Does the phone make voices sound all right?		
5. Do you like the sound of the ring?		
6. Does the cord look sturdy?		
7. Does the manufacturer have a good reputation?		
8. Can you return the phone after trying it at home?		
9. Is there at least a year's warranty?		
10. Is repair easy to arrange?		

---

*There really was such an organization. It was founded around 1960 to protest Ma Bell's decision to convert all the old letter exchanges to pure numbers. One of the society's leading members was none other than S.I. Hayakawa, the famed semanticist and former U.S. Senator from California. We called Dr. Hayakawa at his home in Mill Valley, California, and heard him tell how the Anti-Digit Dialing League had tried to fight the phone company.

"Our headquarters was the 'no name bar' in Sausalito," Hayakawa recalled. At one of its press conferences, the League fielded a line of bathing beauties with banners bearing the names of several famous San Francisco telephone exchanges—EVergreen, PRospect, BAyview, and LOmbard—across their fronts. But, in retrospect, Hayakawa thinks the whole campaign was just "spitting into the gale. Now that we can use numerals to direct-dial Singapore and Kenya, I yield," he says magnanimously.

store to test different equipment, he finally selected one loaded with features and headed home. Plugging in the new phone in the master bedroom, he thought his job was done. But that was before the new phone rang that afternoon during his wife's nap with such a high-pitched shriek that she was awakened from her sleep screaming that a fire alarm had gone off.

When it comes to repair problems, cords are the Achilles' heel of telephones. Frayed and damaged cords are responsible for a third of all telephone problems. They have a knack of getting caught in doors, pulling loose at the plug, and being chewed on by babies. Insist on a phone with a heavy-duty cord and be sure that there are modular plugs where the cord connects to both the wall and receiver so that defective cords can be replaced easily. Unless you're buying a "disposable phone" that you're prepared to throw away at the first sign of trouble, avoid phones with what the industry calls "skinny-wire" cords that are "hard-wired" to the receiver instead of being attached in modular fashion.

Keep in mind that the more expensive the phone you're buying, the more important the warranty and repair considerations will be to you, should it break. After purchasing an expensive phone, you won't want to have to sell your house just to keep the phone in repair.

CHAPTER 3 Telephone Equipment Features

In the days before computer chips, telephones were built with electromechanical rather than electronic parts. All the wires, screws, and switches made the old electromechanical models big and bulky, but they lasted forever. In at least one Maine community, you still can find people using hand-cranked phones of pre-World War I vintage.

Phones today are going electronic. Computer chips make it both cheaper and easier to design phones with things like automatic redial and special speaker features. If properly engineered, electronic phones should be at least as reliable as their electromechanical counterparts. But there's a big difference between the type of electronics needed for a quality phone and the circuitry that went into the millions of cheap disposable phones imported from Asia a couple of years ago. The moral is, don't automatically shy away from electronic phones because of their bad reputation, but generally expect to get what you pay for.

Pulse- vs. Tone-Dialing

A key question for anyone buying a phone today is whether to choose a phone that operates on pulse- or touch-tone-dialing. Your decision may have a major effect on both your long-distance bill and other calling habits.

Telephones with rotary-dials—which includes half of the nation's phones—pulse-dial. As the dial is spun, a pulse is sent along the line, one per digit. In touch-tone dialing each digit on the dial is represented by different musical tones. When a call is made, the musical notes transmitted down the line let the telephone company know which number is being called. No prior musical training is needed, of course.

CAN YOU NAME THIS TUNE?

9636999-666-900

96369999666963

Many people think any telephone with push button keys provides touch-tone dialing. But some push button telephones today imitate the pulses of rotary-dial models. If you're not sure which mode a phone follows, look at the FCC registration code on the bottom of the phone. The last letter of the code will be either *T* for tone, *R* for rotary or pulse, or *E* for either. Phones with an *E* will have a switch somewhere on the phone to allow you to shift back and forth between pulse and tone.

If all this sounds a little academic, there's a bottom line, we assure you. Until "equal access" comes to your community and you have the capability to dial any long-distance carrier as easily as AT&T, you'll need a touch-tone phone if you wish to use any of the discount long-distance services such as MCI or GTE Sprint. Depending on your calling habits, the savings from such services can be considerable. (For more on discount long-distance services and how they work, see Chapter 10.)

Between now and the fall of 1986, some 70 percent of American households will be converted to equal access. Once your exchange gets equal access, you'll be able to use any long-distance company you want, even with a rotary phone. If you're only an occasional long-distance caller, there may be very little economic sense to buying touch-tone phones, now. First, it usually costs at least $10 more to buy tone than rotary phones. Second, local phone companies sometimes impose one-time fees as high as $20 to convert your line from rotary- to touch-tone dialing. Third, the local service charges for touch-tone phones in some areas of the country can be more than $2 a month higher than for rotary instruments.

Don't forget, however, that equal access may be many months away for your exchange, and if you make even $10 to $15 a month in long-distance calls, the discount carriers could be saving you money.

From the standpoint of convenience, a touch-tone phone is just faster and easier to use than a rotary-dial phone. In addition, virtually all the new information services such as home banking, home shopping, and stock quote retrieval (see Chapter 17) that will be available to you by phone over the next few years require touch-tone phones. To stay abreast of the future, you'll want at least one touch-tone phone in your home.

Pulse/Tone Switch

If you want to avoid the local telephone company's special line conversion fees and monthly service charges for touch-tone phones, there are phones with a switch that enables you to shift back and forth from pulse to tone. Since calls over one of the alternative long-distance carriers, or to a bank or other computer data bank, always begin with a local call, you can use pulse-dialing for the first leg of your call, then switch to touch-tone dialing as required to complete your transaction.

Another alternative to the pulse/tone problem is to buy a special tone generator that can be screwed into the mouthpiece of a standard rotary phone, thus transforming it into a touch-tone instrument for about $40. At that price you're probably better off buying a new phone.

Hold Feature

Telephone manufacturers tell us that this is one of their customers' favorite options. The hold feature allows you to put a call on hold without losing it while you switch the conversation to an extension phone elsewhere in your home or office. With a hold feature, you can hang up a receiver rather than just leaving it off the hook and making callers listen to you yell, "Horace! The phone's for you. Pick it up in the den!" You also protect against the possibility that some well-intentioned third party may hang up the open receiver while you're on your way to an extension phone in another room, and you spare yourself the need to backtrack to the room you left to make sure the first phone is hung up.

Some hold features work by simply depressing the phone's switchhook rapidly once or twice before hanging up the receiver. Other phones have a little button somewhere on the dialing face to activate the function. Some fancier models will even give you music-on-hold. If you'd like a hold feature but don't want to buy a new phone, you can buy a do-it-yourself kit that will add a hold capability to every extension on your line with very little effort. The kit costs about $15 at any phone store. We've found it to be a very useful option.

Auto-Redial

If you've ever spent half an hour getting nothing but busy signals from the local cab company, your child's pediatrician, or your favorite bookie, you'll appreciate automatic redial. An auto-redial phone has a built-in computer "memory" that remembers the last number called. By pushing a button or two, you can direct the phone to redial that number automatically every thirty or forty seconds for a specified period of time. If someone answers at the other end, your phone will ring you back so that you will know that your call has gone through and you should pick up the receiver if you wish to talk. Instead of dialing the telephone *ad nauseam*, you can spend your time reading a good book.

Last-Number Dial

The poor man's version of auto-redial, last-number dial works in much the same way as auto-redial, but you have to push the special redial button on your phone each time you wish to try the number. The phone won't keep redialing it for you automatically. LND is often found in even the cheapest disposable phones. You should be aware that the number of dialing digits that can be "remembered" by many of the cheaper phones is often less than a dozen. While that's enough to redial a standard local or long-distance number, it is not enough to add either a credit card number or access code for one of the alternative long-distance carriers into the number you are redialing. Unfortunately, to everyone's confusion, last-number dial is also sometimes referred to as auto-redial.

Memory or Speed-Dialing

A close kin to auto-redial, phones with memory or speed-dialing allow you to store your most frequently used numbers in the phone's memory so that you can call them by just pressing a button or two. Depending on the model, you may be able to store anywhere from eight or nine such numbers to as many as a couple of hundred.

If you use a long-distance service with access codes that require a lot of extra dialing, you can program in the access codes for speed-dialing. Some phones will even let you program in a pause in your dialing. This is important when you're dialing a long-distance carrier like MCI because there's always a second or two after you've made your call to the company's local switch before the carrier can request the access code that qualifies you to connect with the network and complete your call. While you'll still be able to use your speed-dialer for calling on the alternative long-distance services, the process is likely to require extra steps unless your phone is equipped to permit a pause in the dialing process. Until you've actually tried a phone's pause feature out yourself, don't assume it works. This is an area where promise and performance don't always match.

The speed-dial capability can be added to a phone you already own or lease with a special "automatic dialer" attachment for sale in most phone specialty stores.

Speaker Phones

Otherwise known as "squawk boxes," speaker phones are great for holding conference calls when you need to include several persons in the conversation at your end of the line. Even more helpful, speaker phones leave you free to do other things with your hands while talking, such as leafing through a file, taking notes, or gesturing as expressively as a New York cab driver when you don't like what's being said on the other end of the line. The parties you're talking to may not be able to see your gestures, but at least you get the psychic satisfaction of making them.

Before you buy a squawk box, you should always test its sound quality using a variety of voices. You don't want to sound as if you're speaking from the bottom of the well. Be especially careful of phones that combine their speaker feature with a clock-radio. All too often you can hear the radio playing when you're using the speaker phone.

Two-line Phones

A standard feature in some offices, the two-line phone in the home has long been seen as one of those things that make the rich different from you and us. But telephone industry competition has brought the price of two-line phones down to as low as $70. While that's still more than the cost of a basic single-line phone, it's a small price, we think, for not having to queue up to use the phone in your own home, anymore, and for not having to worry that an important business contact or personal caller can't get through to you because your teenager is chewing on the horn with a friend. If you're a doctor, lawyer, or other professional, or have an office at home, the case becomes even more compelling.

Personal computer owners with both the equipment (see Chapter 17) and interest in sending and receiving computer data over the phone lines will also be prime candidates for two-line phones. Getting a second line and reserving it for computer communications is the only way to insure that when your computer is "on-line" with a remote data bank, you won't lose your connection, should someone pick up a phone extension elsewhere in the house.

A two-line phone isn't the only way to field two incoming calls at once. You may also live in a service area where Call Waiting is available as an option from your local telephone company for a few additional dollars each month. With Call Waiting, the local operating company will send several clicks across your line while you're talking, to indicate when a second caller is trying to reach you. By executing a simple procedure with your switch-hook, you can put your first caller on hold and take the second call, or you can ignore the second caller and hope that he or she will call back.

For many families, Call Waiting is a good alternative to buying your own two-line phones. But remember, Call Waiting only helps you manage incoming calls. If you and a friend are discussing movie schedules over the phone, and you want to put your friend on hold while you call a theater to check a time, Call

Waiting won't help you. You'll need a two-line phone. Before signing up for Call Waiting, you should also realize that some telephone users find the clicking sounds of Call Waiting on the line so rattling that they forget what they are saying.

Installing a two-line phone takes a little more effort than a single-line instrument, but even so, it's no big deal. For instructions on how to do it, see Chapter 6.

The World Is Your Oyster

Believe it or not, what we have outlined above is just the beginning of your options. The bells and whistles available to you in the Brave New World are nearly endless. Here, in summary form, are just a few:

- Intercom, to allow you to speak to another extension on the line.
- Page, which is similar to Intercom, except that your voice goes out over an external public address system rather than your telephone when you want to send a message.
- Ringer-silencer switch, which enables you to kill your telephone's ring if you wish.
- Amplified phones, for noisy rooms or the hard-of-hearing. For more information on telephone equipment for the physically handicapped, call the AT&T National Special Needs Center, 800-233-1222. If you want information on Telecommunications Devices for the Deaf, call 800-833-3232.
- Priority code, a software option that lets you program your phone so that only persons with a special code can reach you on your line.

In Section 5, there are a variety of other useful and exciting options to choose from. For the lowdown on answering machines, cordless and cellular phones, and devices to enable your personal computer to "talk" to a variety of electronic information banks over the telephone lines, we suggest you read on.

SECTION

2

Installation and Repair

"IT'S REALLY SIMPLE, EDNA. THE PHONE COMPANY WILL MAINTAIN EVERYTHING
OUTSIDE THE HOUSE ... YOU PAY FOR ANYTHING INSIDE!"

CHAPTER 4 Do-It-Yourself and Save

W e have a friend who refuses to try to work on anything that has wires connected to it. "The two things I don't understand," he says firmly, "are my spouse and electricity." We offer no counsel on spouses, but we say with confidence that anyone able to follow simple directions can do his own home telephone wiring. That includes everything from changing a telephone jack to moving an extension telephone or adding the interior wiring for a second phone line to his house or apartment. It also includes simple repairs.

Why, you may ask, would anyone want to do that? Why not just call the phone company? Simple. To save money. As a result of all the legal changes in the telephone system, you now own the telephone wires inside your house, just as you have always owned the electric wires and the water pipes. It costs plenty to get someone to work on those wires. Just to get your friendly local phone company—you know, the one that used to come for free—to call and change a $2.19 phone jack could cost you an arm and a leg. In the District of Columbia, for example, Chesapeake & Potomac Telephone charges $21 for the first quarter-hour and $11 for each fifteen minutes thereafter, plus materials, to work on your interior wiring.

There is no doubt your local telephone company does a fine job of installing telephones and moving extensions. But once you get your courage up, you can do as well, just for the price of materials. Adding an extension phone is a good deal easier than many other household tasks, say, for example, unclogging a stubborn drain pipe. When we have a stubborn clog, we call a plumber who has specialized equipment and the skill to open up our sewer. But when we have a telephone job to do, we can do it ourselves. Residential telephone systems are not nearly as hard to work on as residential plumbing systems.

It is not dangerous to your health, to your house, or to your telephone to work on it yourself. Only if you have been equipped with a heart pacemaker should you avoid attempting to rewire your phone system. Telephones operate on low electrical current, so you can't get shocked—unless you are holding onto the bare telephone wires exactly at the moment someone tries to call your number. If you take the phone off the hook when you're working on it, you can't get tingled by the jingle. However, even if you should make a terrible wiring mistake, you can't set fire to your house. The worst thing you can do to a telephone instrument itself is render it impotent, and we include a troubleshooting guide in Chapter 7 to help you in this regard. It's hard to wreck a telephone, unless you do something truly drastic like driving over it with your car.

All Telephone Systems Are Not the Same

If your phone system was installed before 1973, your phones are probably wired solidly to their outlets ("hard-wired") or connected with bulky four-pronged plugs. Plugs and jacks used by the Bell Telephone System—AT&T and all its affiliated local telephone companies—were not the same as those once used by General Telephone. Fortunately, however, all new phone installations have standard, Federal Communications Commission-approved plugs and jacks, so you can unplug any new phone and move it to another room—or carry it with you to another residence at the other end of the country—and plug it into a standard jack. All modern residential phone equipment, including the instruments, answering machines, computer modems, and other accessories use the same style plugs and jacks, so everything can be connected together.

The new plugs on the ends of telephone cords are called "modular." AT&T calls them "pinch plugs." They are miniature, rectangular, plastic devices with a tiny lever on one side that you "pinch" in order to release the plug. On the other side, you can see four or six copper contacts. These plugs snap into the modular jacks in the walls of your home and in the back of your telephone. You have to press the tiny lever to get the plug out. If you have an older home or apartment, you will probably want to change your old-style jacks to modular so you can plug in your own phones, rather than continue to pay a large monthly rental for AT&T's old models.

These tiny jacks and plugs have been cleverly designed to serve more than one purpose, depending upon how they are wired. Most of the time you will not need to know anything about that. But if you decide to add a second telephone line to your residence—something we explain how to do in Chapter 6— it will become very important to understand some of the differences. Since it only takes two wires to operate a single residen-

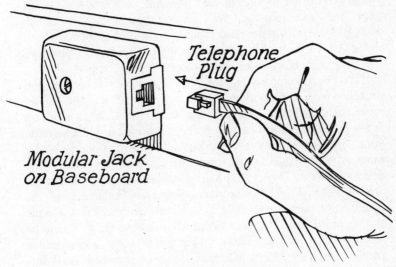

Figure 1. Modular plug and jack

tial phone line, modular jacks with only two wires connected are designated RJ11. If, however, four wires are hooked up in the same jack—so that you can have two different phone lines serving one instrument—it is designated RJ14. For now, just remember that the jacks and plugs can do more than just hook single-line phones and accessories together and to the telephone network.

Look at Your Telephone System

It is helpful to take a careful look at your entire telephone system. It is really quite simple. Start by finding where the phone company's property ends and yours begins; in other words, where the so-called "demarcation point" is. A telephone "drop"—the line from the street—runs to a "station protector," a device that shunts heavy electric current to the ground, rather than into you or your telephone if the phone line is hit by lightning. The station protector is often located in the basement, just inside the point where the drop from the street reaches the house. It is usually black plastic with copper posts that are connected to the telephone wires. A separate heavy wire leads to a ground, often a cold-water pipe. The station protector belongs to the phone company.

If the phone company has worked on your wiring recently, you probably have a network interface jack located near the station protector. A network interface jack is just a modular jack with a fancy name because it serves as the demarcation point between your wires and the phone company's. Your wiring begins with a modular plug plugged into the network interface jack. Many residences, however, do not have a network interface jack. Their wires are connected directly to the station protector. In those cases, the demarcation point, technically, is at the modular jack closest to the station protector. If you are doing extensive rewiring, it may be worthwhile to get the phone company to come and install a network interface jack. You're going to get one, eventually. With a network interface jack in place, you can hook up your phones almost any way you wish. Otherwise, you may be tempted to hook your own phone lines directly to the station protector. That's what the telephone installer did in the past, of course, but that's now technically not allowed. You may wish to ask your local phone company if it cares if you install a network interface jack, yourself. Although you are not supposed to put in your own network interface jack, some companies say they don't mind if you do it yourself. "You can do it cheaper than we can do it for you," the spokesman for one local company explained.

The telephone cable that runs through your house from the station protector or the network interface jack contains four or six wires inside a plastic outer covering. The wires are color-coded so you can keep track of them. The color codes are more or less standard. If you have a four-conductor cable, the wires are red, green, yellow, and black. Line one is connected to red and green; line two can be connected to black and yellow. In most residences with a single telephone line, only the red and green wires are used. In a residence with a single line, the black and yellow wires can also be used to supply power from a transformer to phones with lighted dials. In telephony, red is the "ring" or negative side of the direct current circuit, while green is the "tip" or positive side. If you have a six-conductor line, the colors are blue with a white band, white with a blue band, orange with a white band, white with an orange band, green with a white band, and white with a green band. Here is how they match:

TABLE 3

	4-WIRE	6-WIRE
Line 1	RED	BLUE WITH WHITE BAND
	GREEN	WHITE WITH BLUE BAND
Line 2	YELLOW	ORANGE WITH WHITE BAND
	BLACK	WHITE WITH ORANGE BAND
Line 3		GREEN WITH WHITE BAND
		WHITE WITH GREEN BAND

The cables run from the network interface jack to terminal blocks or modular jacks. These are points where the cable wires are screwed into something you can plug a telephone into. Sometimes your telephone cables connect to junction boxes along the way. Junction boxes are central connecting points for telephone wiring. One pair of wires goes into them, and two, three or four pairs of wires come out.

The whole point of doing your own telephone work is to save money. In order to save money, however, you need to spend just a little at the beginning to buy some useful tools. While it is possible to wire an entire building using only your trusty Swiss army knife, you won't want to do that. With such a hefty tool you can nick a wire and weaken it when you scrape the insulation off. What you really need is a $3.95 telephone wire stripper. This handy-dandy little gadget is almost as great as the vegetable choppers advertised on television. The telephone-wire stripper, available in most phone stores including those operated by AT&T, is used to strip insulation off the telephone

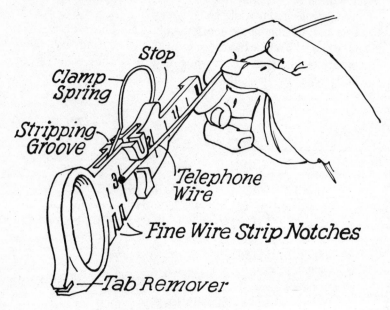

Figure 2. Telephone Wire Stripper

wire in an exceptionally neat, easy fashion. Not only that, it includes, at the same low $3.95 price, a ruler and a nifty staple holder so you won't smash your finger or drive a staple through the phone line, shorting it. If you hit your finger with a hammer only once while stapling phone wire in place, you'll realize it was stupid not to have purchased the telephone wire stripper. Some telephone wire strippers, including those sold by AT&T, don't have two little metal notches for stripping the insulation off the fine conducting wires. Be sure the telephone wire stripper you buy has those two little notches.

_____ TABLE 4 _____
Tools Needed for Jobs

Required:
Standard screwdriver
Phillips-head screwdriver
Telephone wire stripper
Optional:
Hammer
Needle-nosed pliers
Wire cutters
Electric or hand drill, with drill bits
Staple gun, staples
Stud finder
Tape measure
Electrical tape
Chisel
Keyhole saw
Plastic safety glasses

For any job, large or small, you'll need a standard screwdriver and a Phillips-head screwdriver. Good-quality screwdrivers are cheap, and you'll regret it if you buy twenty-nine-cent models out of a barrel in a hardware store. Crummy screwdrivers can wreck screws—and otherwise make your job needlessly difficult. We can't imagine a household that doesn't need screwdrivers for all sorts of other tasks, anyway, so get good ones. Along with screwdrivers, you may need wire-cutting pliers, although if all you have to cut is new telephone wire, you may be able to get by with big scissors, if the scissors aren't too high-quality. (Cutting wire with a really fine pair of shears could damage the shears seriously.) The wire stripper, screwdrivers, and some kind of wire cutter are essential. Depending on the job, you may also need a drill and drill bits (including a special Bell hanger bit), staples, tape measure, electrical tape, hammer, chisel, needle-nosed pliers, keyhole saw, and, of course, various modular jacks, fasteners, and telephone wire. A stud finder—a little magnet that can pivot in a transparent plastic case and point at nails under the paint and plaster—can be useful for locating the studs in a wall. It is also a good idea to wear a pair of plastic safety glasses (they are cheap) if you use an electric drill or other power tool.

Some experts say they recommend wearing rubber gloves to work on telephone circuits, as protection against possible electric shocks. We don't think rubber gloves are necessary or even desirable. The threat of shock from a telephone circuit is slim. And we're not sure how you could hook up small wires while wearing rubber gloves, anyway.

All the tools and materials you need to work on your telephone system are widely available. You can find them at any phone store and at most department and hardware stores. Radio Shack and other electronics stores usually have excellent supplies of telephone parts. Before you set out to do a serious job, we strongly advise visiting a well-stocked store to look at all the wonderful phone jacks and plugs, cords, and other devices.

If you plan your work, follow our suggestions in the next few chapters, and use a modest amount of care, you'll be able to tackle virtually any residential telephone wiring and installation jobs. You'll save a lot of money—and you'll get the job done the way you want it done. Of course, there's always the chance you could run into an unusual situation or face a problem that seems insoluble. Don't worry. Use your telephone to find the answer to your unusual problem. Call AT&T's hot line, 800-222-3111, any time, day or night, twenty-four hours a day. An expert will talk you through.

CHAPTER 5 Converting Old-style Plugs to Modular

It can be downright embarrassing to buy a new telephone—and then discover that the phone outlets in your residence won't accept the new phone. This chapter tells you how to change the outlets in your home so you can plug in your new phone. These simple directions are all most people will ever have to know about telephone wiring.

All new phones require "modular" jacks and plugs. Grab your present telephone cord firmly and follow it to the point where it enters the wall. If your telephone cord plugs into a small rectangular hole about a quarter of an inch across and three-eighths of an inch high, you're lucky; you already have modular jacks. If your telephone cord has a bulky, four-pronged plug on the end, you're not quite so lucky, but you don't have a big job making changes. If your telephone cord just disappears into a round hole or into a terminal box, you'll need to do a little simple wiring.

With modular jacks (jacks are the sockets into which you put the plugs), you remove the rented phone by squeezing the little plastic lever on the plug and yanking gently. Plug your new phone into the same jack. You should hear or feel the plug snap into place. If your new phone has a switch for pulse- or tone-dialing, set it to the service you have. Lift the receiver to hear the dial tone. Call a friend and tell them about your new phone. That's all there is to it.

It is only slightly more complicated to change a wall phone that has a modular plug. Take the receiver off the hook to get it out of the way, and push up on the rental telephone. It should slip off two mounting studs and come free. Sometimes you must hit the bottom of the phone with the palm of your hand to pop it free. You can see that your phone was attached to a plate that is fastened to the wall. The wall mount has a modular jack in the middle and two mounting studs, top and bottom. Look at the back of your new wall phone. There are two slots for the mounting studs and there is a modular plug sticking out. Notice that the plug can slide up and down a short distance. Slide the plug all the way to the bottom and, by maneuvering the phone, stick the plug into the jack on the wall. Make sure the studs on the wall mount are in the two slots. Pull the phone down firmly until it is in position. As before, set the phone for pulse- or tone-dialing, lift the receiver, and call a friend.

Convert a Four-Pronged Outlet

If your rental telephones have plugs with four prongs, it is not hard to convert the existing outlets to accept modular plugs. The simplest way is to stick four-prong-to-modular cord adaptors into the existing four-prong jacks. Then insert the modular plugs into the modular jacks on the cord adaptors. The adaptors cost about $4 or less and require no tools to install.

If your present phones are hard-wired to their outlets, you'll have to change the outlets. Follow the cord to the point where it enters a small box, often on the baseboard. A telephone repairman calls this a "42A block." You want to convert the 42A block to a modular jack.

To this point, you have just been plugging cords into jacks, which is no more dangerous than plugging an electric cord into an outlet. But since you are now going to work directly on your telephone wires, it is time to take a few simple precautions. If you have a heart pacemaker, stop immediately, sip a glass of iced tea, and call the telephone company or an independent contractor to do your wiring. Don't work on your telephones during a thunderstorm. If any of your telephones have lighted dials or buttons, that means voltage is being supplied to some of the wires in your telephone circuit from a small transformer that is plugged into the electrical system. Find the transformer and unplug it. Finally, just before you begin work, take the phone off-hook (that's telephone talk for taking the receiver off its cradle). That way the phone is "busy" and can't ring while you're working on it. The ring is produced by a higher voltage on the phone line—enough to give you a little shock. Ignore the phone company's recorded messages reminding you to hang up the phone. Place a pillow over the receiver if necessary to drown out the sound.

The easiest way to convert a 42A block to a modular jack is with a universal instant jack. Remove the single screw that holds the cover on the 42A block. Here you may run into trouble if someone has painted the cover along with the walls. If the groove in the screw is filled with old paint, clean it out before you try to remove the screw. Use one corner of the screwdriver like a chisel. Place it in the screw groove at an angle and tap the screwdriver gently with a hammer. The paint should come out so you can remove the screw.

With the 42A block cover off, you can see the four screws inside that connect wires from the telephone circuit to the telephone cord. Pull on the cord gently so you can see where each wire is connected. Now it's time for your first telephone surgery. Take a deep breath and grasp a small wire cutter firmly in your hand. Snip each of the wires connecting the cord to the block. Cut the wires close to the screws, taking care not to cut the other wires that lead off into the wall somewhere.

Place the universal instant jack over the 42A block and, using the screw that came with it, tighten it down. The electrical connection is made with little springs that touch the screws in the 42A, so you don't have to do any wiring. Plug in your phone and make a call. If

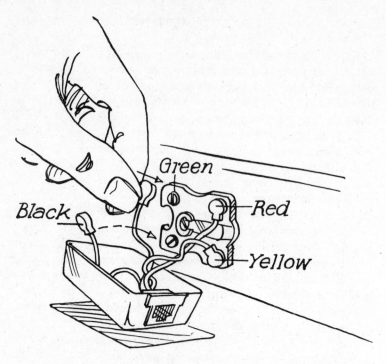

Figure 3. 42A to Modular with Snap-on Connectors

the phone doesn't work, unplug the phone, remove the jack, rotate the jack half a turn, and tighten it again. It should work.

Another easy way to convert a 42A block is with modular jacks that use snap-on connectors. Remove the cover of the 42A block and cut the old phone cord wires as explained above. Each snap-on connector is a different bright color, to correspond with the color codes used in telephone wires. Most likely, your residence has four-conductor telephone cable. Each of the four little wires in the cable is a different color, red, green, yellow, and black. In Chapter 4 we identified what each color means—or what you do if your house has six-conductor cable, with an entirely different color scheme. For now, snap the red conductor on the screw with the red wire, the green on the green, the yellow on the yellow, and the black on the black. Screw the new cover into the old 42A block, plug in your telephone, and make a call. If you get a dial tone but you can't

54

"break" it by dialing numbers, don't panic. That's a common installation problem. You just need to switch the red and green wires around. Then the phone will work just fine.

Modular Jacks

A variety of modular jacks can be wired to a 42A block or used in place of it, in addition to those described above. Visit a phone store and look at them to see if one or another fits your installations or your tastes more closely. For example, there are modular jacks with four short, color-coded wires leading from them. At the end of each wire is a "spade lug," a half-moon-shaped bit of metal. To connect spade lugs, loosen each screw on the 42A block in turn, insert the spade lug on the red wire under the screw holding the red wire, the green on the green, etc. Take care to insure that the shank on one lug is not touching another. That could short the circuit.

Some four-prong telephone jacks are mounted in outlet boxes similar to those that contain electric sockets. Some hard-wired

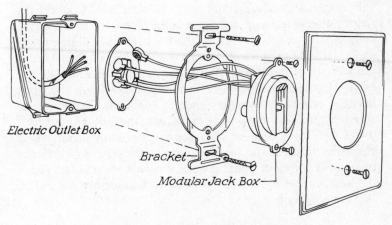

Figure 4. Electric outlet boxes

telephone cords go through a hole in the faceplate of an outlet box to a 42A block mounted inside. Both can be converted to modular jacks. Remove the faceplate. Inside you'll find either a bracket holding the four-prong jack in place or a 42A block. If there is a bracket, remove the screws holding it. Pull the bracket away from the outlet box so you can see the four telephone wires screwed to the back of the four-prong jack. Carefully loosen the screws holding each of the wires. If you have a 42A block in the outlet box, loosen the screws to remove the wires from both the telephone cord and the residential cable. In either case, you should now have four loose telephone wires.

Go to a phone or other store that sells telephone hardware and buy a modular jack assembly that can fit into a standard outlet box. You will be able to choose from several styles. We recommend that you buy an assembly that has two outlets. It looks something like the familiar electrical outlet, as it should, for it fits into the same outlet box. There are a couple of reasons why two outlets are better than one. First, of course, you can plug in two different phones, or one phone and a telephone device, such as an answering machine or a modem for a computer. Second, if you decide at some point to add a second telephone line, you can make one jack line 1 and the second jack line 2 by moving wires to different connections. The directions that come with the jack show you how to do it.

For now, let's assume you have only one line. Connect the red wire to the red wire, the green to the green, the yellow to the yellow, the black to the black. The connections will be easy to make if the house wires already have spade lugs on them. If you are working with bare wires, make a small hook at the end of each. Needle-nosed pliers are handy for this. Slip the hook between two of the washers under a connecting screw. Make sure the open part of the hook is facing to the right as you slip it under the screw, because screws are tightened by turning them clockwise. If the hooks face left, turning the screws could force the wires to slip out from between the washers. Finally, install the new bracket to hold the modular jack assembly and put on the new faceplate.

Wall Telephones

Replacing an old-style wall telephone with a modular wall phone is somewhat more difficult than changing wall jacks. First you must remove the old telephone from the wall. This is usually a two-step process. Find the notch in the bottom of the wall phone's cover. Poke a screwdriver or the eraser end of a pencil into the notch to release the phone cover. Set the cover aside. Now find the two screws, top and bottom, that hold the telephone itself to the wall. Loosen the screws. Lift the phone away from the wall. You'll find that the phone is still connected to four wires that often come from an outlet box right behind the wall phone. Sometimes, however, the telephone cable is stapled to the wall. Either loosen the screws that connect the wires to the phone or cut them next to the screws with wire cutters.

Examine the telephone cable that led to the wall phone. Note that it contains four small color-coded insulated wires encased in a plastic sheath. You should remove enough of the sheath so that the small wires—still in their own insulation—stick out about three inches. While you could remove the sheath with your Swiss army knife or a paring knife from the kitchen, you'd do much better with your new telephone wire stripper. Use the three-inch ruler on the stripper to figure out how much of the outer sheath to remove. Lift the wire spring of the stripper and insert the telephone cable into the stripping groove right to the point where you wish to cut off the outer covering. Close the clamp spring of the stripper. Stick your finger into the hole at the end of the stripper and rotate it around the wire several times. The little knife in the stripper circumcises the sheath without damaging the four wires inside. With the clamp spring still closed, pull the cable through the groove to remove the sheath.

You will have to buy a modular wall mounting plate. There are two types, each costing $7 or less, and both accept the same phones. With the first, you connect the four conductor wires to screws on the backplate. Start by stripping about an inch of insulation off each of the conductor wires. Use the handy-dandy telephone-wire stripper, of course. Find the connecting terminals in the wall phone modular jack. Fasten the red wire to R1, the green wire to T1, the black wire to AUX, and the yellow wire to GN.

With the second type of modular wall-mounting plate, you first take the faceplate off and set it aside. Then feed the cable through the rear of the backplate and fasten the plate to the outlet box or the wall. Place the four conductor wires into grooves in two plastic connector caps, red wire in position 2, black in position 4, green in position 1, and yellow in position 3. It is not necessary to strip the insulation from the four conductor wires for this installation—although you can if you wish—because the connectors will cut through the insulation when the connector caps are pushed on. Using a screwdriver, lever the connector caps with their individual wires onto connectors on the backplate. The wires will be forced into the correct positions. Replace the faceplate. Mount your new modular wall phone.

Many new phones that look as though they are made to sit on a desk can actually double as wall phones. Some of them fit right onto the standard modular wall mounting plates. Another type of phone comes with directions to show you how to take the bottom off the phone case and, perhaps, reverse it so you can mount the phone on the wall.

Now go around your house and look at all your new phones. Just think of how much money you have saved by doing it yourself.

CHAPTER 6 Adding Extension Telephones

B ack in the bad old days, you had a telephone somewhere in your home, maybe in the front hall. That's where you had to go in order to make all your calls, whether it was convenient or not. Then your friendly local telephone company offered to add an extra telephone to your line so you could have another phone in a more convenient place, perhaps the kitchen or your bedroom. You were happy to have the second phone—and the phone company was doubly happy to rent you the extra instrument forever and ever.

Guess what? Forever is over. Now that you can own your own telephones, you can put them anywhere you wish, within the bounds of safety, good sense, and the limits of the phone system. Since all new phones plug straight into modular jacks, you can have phone jacks all over the house. You may not need a phone all the time in your workshop. But when you decide to work there, you can carry a phone to the workshop, plug it in, and be content in the knowledge that you won't miss any important calls. Similarly, you'll rarely need a phone in the guest bedroom. But when Grandma and Grandpa come to visit, it's nice to give them a phone to use.

Adding extension phones wherever you wish is only the beginning. You can add a second telephone line as well. You probably don't know it, but you already have all the inside wiring needed to add a second line to every modular jack in your home. This is because the telephone cable running through your walls contains four or six wires—and you need only two wires for a single line. The other two or four wires have been hiding there all those years, waiting to be discovered and put to use. Once you get the phone company to run a second line to your house, you can do the interior wiring, yourself. It's not even hard, as we'll show you. Already about 7 percent of all American households have a second telephone line, many of them used for teen-aged children, home businesses, or personal computers. (See Chapter 17.) Folks in the telephone equipment business are betting that percentage will skyrocket. Lawrence Reichenstein, vice-president of Webcor, a maker of two-line residential phones, says, "Within five years anyone who's making a decent income will have two lines in his home, one for data, one for voice."

Before you take the grand step of adding a second phone line, however, you'll want to install all the extra modular jacks and extension phones you think you'll need. We're going to assume here that you have already replaced, if necessary, all the old-style jacks in your house and that you've read through Chapter 5 how to do that.

Although you can install as many jacks as you wish, there is a limit to the number of phones you can hang onto a single phone line. The limit is determined by the amount of electrical current the phone company sends down the line to make your phones ring. If you plug too many phones into your line, they may not ring. Your telephone directory may tell you that you are limited to five phones or other telephone devices like answering machines and computer modems on a single line. That's true only if you use five standard telephones that have a "ringer equivalence number" of one each. You need to add up the ringer equivalence numbers (REN) of all the phones and other devices on your line to make sure the total doesn't exceed five. Count each old standard phone you have as one REN. For new phones, look at the Federal Communications Commission tag on the bottom. The REN is listed there.

Smart phones with lots of electronic innards typically take less than one REN to ring. Some have a REN as low as .4. If all your phones have a REN of .4, for example, you could have a dozen separate phones on your line (5 REN divided by .4 equals 12.5). Incidentally, under FCC rules, you are supposed to call your local telephone company every time you add a new phone, modem, or other phone device to your line and tell them the ringer equivalence number. We once actually met someone who did this.

Move a Telephone

Moving or adding telephones can be as simple as plugging a cord into a jack, or it can be more complex, with holes to drill and cables to thread through walls. If you have a modular phone jack and you wish to plug a telephone device such as a modem into the same jack, go to your phone store and buy a duplex or modular T jack. Stick the T jack into the existing outlet and suddenly you have two jacks where before you had just one.

If you have a modular wall jack at one point in a room and you want to locate the telephone someplace else, it is only slightly more difficult than plugging in the T jack. Start by measuring the distance from the existing jack to the point where you wish to have your phone. Let's say the distance is about twenty-five feet. Purchase a twenty-five-foot phone cord that has a modular plug at one end and spade lugs at the other, a surface-mount modular jack, and staples designed to be used with your $3.95 telephone wire stripper. Select staples made for telephone wire that are the same color as the new cord. Despite what some may tell you, do not buy insulated staples. They are unnecessary, hard to use, and ugly. The telephone company's installers do not use insulated staples.

Start by connecting the four spade lugs, one to each conductor wire, to the new modular jack. The red wire goes to the red wire, green to green, yellow to yellow, black to black. Plug the

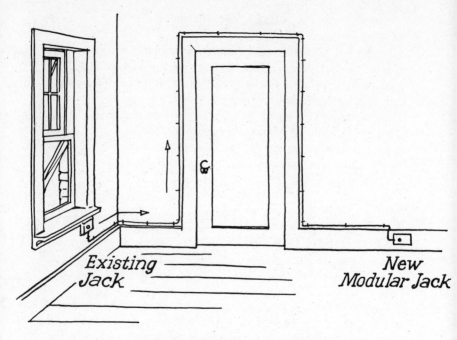

Figure 5. Cable run in a room

other end of the cord into the existing modular jack. Pull the cord straight down from the jack to the baseboard. Fasten the cord to the baseboard with a staple. Be sure to leave a slight amount of slack in the wire so there is no stress on the plug.

Run the cord along the top of the baseboard, stapling it every seven to twelve inches, to the point where you want the new modular jack. Fasten the jack to the baseboard with screws that came with the jack. Drill holes for the screws. Take care to align the modular jack with the baseboard before you drill. If you install the jack on the baseboard crookedly, the phone will work but the jack will look awful.

But, you ask, how do I pound in the staples so I don't smash my fingers, bash the walls with my hammer, or, most importantly, short the cord by stapling through the insulation? These are not trivial questions. Doing a safe, neat stapling job is one of the harder tasks of telephone wiring. But thanks to your amazing $3.95 telephone wire stripper tool, you can look like a stapling expert. Stick a staple partway into the notch at the long, thin end of the wire stripper. There is a groove on the underside of the stripping tool by the staple notch. Place the groove over the telephone wire to position the staple so you don't puncture the wire. Hold the wire stripper in place with your thumb—which you position behind the guard that is, appropriately enough, labeled "thumb." That will keep your fingers a safe distance from your swinging hammer. With the staple in the notch, the wire stripper tool positioned appropriately over the wire, and your thumb safely behind the thumb guard, tap the staple with a hammer. Hit the staple just hard enough to set it so it won't fall out of the wall. Remove the stripper and then hammer the staple home. Don't pound the staple in as far as you can. Be gentle. You just want to hold the cord in place. You don't want to crush it. Place the staples seven to twelve inches apart, taking care to space them evenly for a neat-looking job. When running the cable around corners, make the curve smooth, and put in a staple about an inch from the corner in both directions.

You don't necessarily have to buy a cord with a modular plug on one end and spade lugs on the other to do this job. You can also use bulk telephone cable. Strip three inches of the outer sheath off the cable and strip an inch of insulation off each of the four conductor wires inside. Take the modular jack off the wall, connect the wires to the four screws on the back, then reinstall the jack. (Remember, take one telephone off the hook while you are working on these wires.) Do the same with the new jack at the other end of the cable. You may have to cut a small notch in the jacks to let the cable come out neatly. The jack may have a "breakout tab" somewhere along the edge. Breakout tabs, as the name suggests, are places that you can break out in order to run cables through. Your handy-dandy telephone-wire stripper has a cut at one end, specifically for this purpose.

You do not always have to run the cable along the top of the baseboard. You can run it under a chair rail or along an inconspicuous groove in the baseboard. If the room has wall-to-wall carpeting, you can easily conceal the cable if you pull the carpeting up slightly along the edge and stuff the cord beneath it. Be sure you don't pull the carpeting completely off the tack strip that holds it in place. You can also lay flat telephone cable, made especially to go under carpeting, across the floor before laying a new rug. If you are running cable in the kitchen you may be able to conceal it by running it inside the cabinets. In a bedroom, you can run the cable through a closet to get it out of sight.

A Phone for the Next Room

But what if you want to put a telephone jack in the next room? You can run an extension from the room that has a telephone, just the way you installed the telephone extension inside a room. You have to drill a small hole in the wall and "fish" the cable through. Don't panic if you drill a hole in the wrong place—unless, of course, you hit a water pipe and keep drilling till you puncture it. It is very easy to patch holes in plaster. Locate the spot where you wish the cable to go through the wall. Measure carefully so you know where the hole that you drill in one room will come out in the other. Make sure you are not trying to drill through a stud. Do this by thumping on the wall. Studs are located where the thumping sounds solid.

If you are running the cable along a baseboard, drill a hole right at the top of the baseboard. You probably don't have a drill bit long enough to go through the wall. You can buy a special Bell hanger bit, made for drilling through walls to install phone lines. They are available at phone stores. Or, if you just need to cut through the plaster on the other side, fashion a makeshift drill bit out of an old coat hanger. Cut out the straight part of the hanger and flatten one end with a hammer to make a cutting edge. To drill through the wall, start by drilling a hole in one side with a standard drill bit. Then put your makeshift hanger bit in the drill's chucks and insert it into the hole you've already made. Hold the drill level to the floor and at a right angle to the wall, and make a hole in the opposite wall. Use a standard drill bit to clean up the hole on the other side.

Now that you have a hole drilled through the wall, you need to "fish" the cable through. The easiest way to do this is to tape the cable end to the end of the clothes hanger wire, poke the wire through the wall, and pull the cable into the next room.

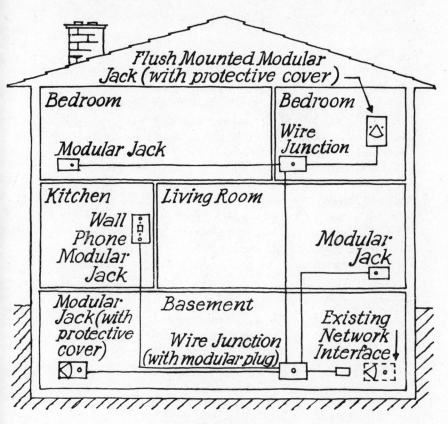

Figure 6. Living plan sketch

Once you've added a simple extension to an existing jack, you're ready to tackle bigger jobs, such as laying more complicated extension lines, and even putting in the wiring for a second phone line. At this point, you should take a long, careful look at your entire telephone system. Draw a rough plan of your residence. Start at the point where the phone line enters your home or apartment—the station protector or the network interface jack— and trace the route of the cables from jack to jack through the attic, wall, and basement. If you can find all the existing wires, or puzzle out where they go through the walls, you will be able to plan your tasks better.

Once you have a plan sketched out, decide where you want extra phone jacks. Look at every room in the house and ask yourself and your family members, "Do we want to put a phone here?" You may end up rejecting some locations because you decide it is too hard to run a line, or for some other reason. But start by considering every possible location for jacks. Don't overlook the patio behind the house. You may want to install a waterproof jack there. With your plan in hand, make a list of parts to get from the phone and hardware stores. Count the number of modular jacks and wire junctions you need, then figure out how much wire to buy. Four-conductor wire costs about $10.95 for one hundred feet, and six-conductor wire costs about $13.95. We can't think of a reason why you would not want to install six-conductor wire. Though you may not need even four wires now, you can't foresee all the wonderful gadgets you'll want to have on the phone system. Be prepared.

_____ **TABLE 5** _____

As you plan your wiring, keep some simple rules in mind.

1. Don't place a phone jack where it will permit a person to use a phone while he's in a bathtub, shower, or swimming pool. You also don't want the phone located where it can be dropped into a sink or toilet.
2. Don't run any wires outside between buildings. They could be hit by lightning.
3. Don't mount a modular jack with the hole at the top. Dust and dirt could fall in.
4. Don't splice telephone wires. They could corrode and fail. Always join wires with modular connectors or wire junction boxes.
5. Avoid damp locations and places such as door and window openings where the wires could be broken or subject to abrasion, as when they are run next to gratings or grillwork. Wrap electrical tape around any wires that could possibly be abraded.
6. Don't place any telephone wire in the same conduits or outlet boxes that contain electrical wiring. Never place phone wiring near bare power wires, lightning rods, antennas, transformers, steam or hot water pipes, or heating ducts.
7. If you are locating a jack near a desk, keep in mind whether the person who uses it most is right- or left-handed.
8. Drill holes in walls very carefully so you don't hit a water pipe or electric cable.

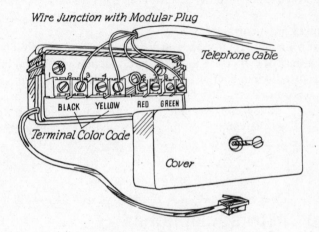

Figure 7. Wire junctions

Additional outlets can be installed by running cables across ceilings and inside walls. Interior walls and ceilings are hollow, so you can hide wires inside them for a neat job. The outer surfaces, usually plasterboard or paneling, are thin; they cover beams, usually two-by-fours.

If you have an open, unfinished basement that contains a modular jack or wire junction, you will have few problems running telephones to any room on the first floor. When you have chosen a location for a baseboard modular jack, drill a hole straight down through the floor. If the floor is carpeted, you can drill right through the rug next to the baseboard. Run the cable through the hole into the basement to the wire junction or a modular jack. Staple the cable to the ceiling beams.

You can simplify your wiring jobs with wire junctions. They are little boxes that serve as central connecting points for telephone wiring. If you want to add, say, three telephone jacks in three rooms on the first floor, run the cables from each to a wire junction in the basement. Then run one cable from the junction to a modular jack—or to another wire junction—to hook it up. It is even easier to hook up a wire junction than a modular jack, because the screws are bigger and the wire code colors are painted brightly enough so you need not worry about hooking it up incorrectly.

You probably already have at least one wire junction if you have a network interface jack. A wire junction with a modular plug is usually found a few inches from the NIJ; a cable from the wire junction box is plugged into the NIJ. Up to four separate telephone cables can emanate from this wire junction. It is handy to run the cable from this wire junction for many extension telephone installations.

Wire Upstairs Telephones

Just as you can run phone cables through an open basement to connect phones on the first floor, you can run phone cables through an attic to upstairs telephones. It is harder to work in an attic than in a basement, however. If there is no floor, you must be careful not to step off the beams. If you don't feel confident maneuvering around your attic, give up and call the phone company. Whatever it costs to have the phone company run the wires is surely less than patching the ceiling where you put your foot through.

The attic poses other extra problems. First, you have to have a telephone cable there to begin with or else bring one in. Second, you have to get cable from the attic to individual rooms, down through the center of walls. Both pose challenges to your skill, cunning, and, as you work under the eaves, your abilities as a contortionist.

If your home doesn't have a telephone cable in the attic, you'll have to figure a way to run a cable from a modular jack or wire junction somewhere to the attic. You could run a cable from a modular jack on the floor below, for example. You could run a cable from the basement through the walls or along the big sewage pipes to the attic. Or you could give up and run a cable on the outside of the house from the basement to the attic.

Often the easiest way to get a cable to the attic is from the floor below. Look around the house for a modular jack that has a closet on the other side of the wall. If you're lucky enough to have one, run a cable from the modular jack through the wall into the closet. Drill a hole in one corner of the closet ceiling into the attic. Run the cable through the ceiling into the attic.

You can run a cable up to the attic from a modular jack in an outlet box on the floor below. This involves some delicate measuring and fishing for cable. In the attic, locate the two-by-four plate at the top of the wall below. Measure carefully to find the spot along the plate that is directly above the outlet box. Bore a three-eighth-inch hole straight down through the two-by-four plate. Tie a heavy weight, such as a couple of loops of solder, on a string and lower it through the hole. As the string with the weight passes by the outlet box below, have a friend fish it out with another wire that has a small hook bent on the end. Then tape the string to the cable end and pull it through.

Once you have a cable to the attic, you can distribute cables from a wire junction to any room below. Follow the same procedure outlined above. Drill a hole, drop a fishing line, and catch the line through a hole drilled just above the baseboard where you will mount the jack. In this case, you may have to drill a slightly larger hole than needed for the wire, in order to fish it through. Repair the hole with patching plaster and a dab of paint.

You can also install an electrical outlet box in the wall and mount your modular jack or jacks in it. It is harder than screwing a modular jack to the baseboard—and not everyone will want to bother. But some like the appearance. Before beginning this job, take a look at the electrical outlets in your home. Mount the telephone outlet box at the same height from the floor, for the sake of appearance. Be sure not to put the modular jack in the same box with electrical wiring.

To mount an outlet box, first find the stud in the wall. You can do this by thumping on the wall with your hand or hunting with a magnetic stud-finder. The little magnet in the transparent plastic box points at nails under the paint that hold the plasterboard to the studs. Where there is a nail, there is a stud. When you think you have found a stud, move a slight distance right or left and drill a small hole about where you want to put the box. Make a 90-degree bend in an eight-inch piece of coat hanger wire and stick it in the hole. By rotating the wire you can find exactly where the stud is located.

You should pick your outlet box to match the kind of walls you have. Since most walls are plasterboard, you'll probably select one that is designed to anchor in the plasterboard. Once you have located the stud, hold the new outlet box up to the wall and draw an outline of it right next to the stud. If your walls are plasterboard, cut along the drawing with a carpenter's utility knife. Be careful not to overshoot the corners and mess up your wall needlessly. When you have cut a neat hole, pull the telephone cable into the new outlet box and insert the box in the wall. When you are finished and have put the cover plate on the outlet, it will look as though it was installed when the house was built.

Now you have modular jacks all over your house. You can have a phone located anyplace you wish. That is very convenient but, you discover, you also need a second telephone line for your computer or your children or your home office. Relax, you don't need to rewire the whole house. You've already done that. Remember, a single phone line takes only two wires, and you have at least four wires running all over the place. All you need to do is call the friendly phone company and ask them to install a second telephone line. They will put a second station protector and a second network interface jack near the one you already have. All you have to do is connect the new phone line to the second pair of wires, the green and black wires that have waited so long to be employed. It's as simple as a visit to a phone store. Ask for a two-line coupler. Radio Shack sells one for $6.95. A two-line coupler is two cables and three plugs, hooked together. Stick the plug for line one into the original network interface jack, the plug for line two into the new NIJ, and the third plug into your wire junction. All of a sudden you have juice to the green and black wires—and every modular jack in the house is suddenly transformed from an RJ11 to an RJ14.

Wonderful, but what does that really mean? It means that all the phones still answer just line one, that's what. In order to use line two, you have to take another step or two. First, you could buy a handful of $6.95 two-line, three-way jacks. They are similar to T-jacks, except that instead of two jacks from one, you get three: line one, line two, and line one and two. With one of these beauties, you can make any phone in the house work on either line one or two—or both. Second, you can buy two-line phones. There are good models for under $100. With a two-line phone, you can answer or call out on either line, put one on hold and answer the other, or even patch the two lines together for a conference call. Third, you can rewire your two-jack outlet boxes so one jack is line one and the second is line two.

With two lines, you can really control your telephone life. You can use line two for the kids' calls, your home business, or your personal computer. Or you could use line two for all your outgoing calls. So you'll never miss an incoming call, you could put an answering machine on line one.

CHAPTER 7
What to Do When Your Phone Breaks

The telephone company used to be like the good old family doctor. It made house calls. A quick call for help from a neighbor's house, and the truck with the Bell insignia came out to fix your phone at no charge. Now, however, the wires that run to your house from the street are maintained by the local phone company, you own the wires inside your house, and you or AT&T own the telephone instruments. If you call the local phone company with a complaint that something is wrong, they'll still come out. But if they discover that the trouble is in *your* telephone instrument and not in *their* lines, they'll bill you for the service visit—$43 in the District of Columbia, more, elsewhere—without fixing the phone. That's not their responsibility anymore. They only do wires.

Today you have the responsibility to fix your phones and the wires inside your house. Only if there is something wrong with the telephone line itself will the local company take responsibility for it. It's up to you to do the preliminary checking necessary to figure out where the problem lies. If it turns out to be something you can't fix, you have to arrange to have someone else do it. That's the bad news. The good news is that phones and internal phone wiring systems seldom break—and when they do they are usually easy to fix. As Harry Newton, publisher of *Teleconnect* magazine, says, "eighty percent of all phone problems can usually be repaired within twenty minutes."

Problems in telephones can develop in any of the following three areas:

- The telephone instruments.
- The interior wiring of your house.
- The telephone company's wiring or equipment.

In most cases, the trouble is in the phone, itself. It can be a ridiculously simple problem. Start by checking to make sure the phone is actually plugged in. Sometimes the new electronic phones go on the blink after sitting in direct sunlight. Park the phone in the shade, let it cool off, and try again later.

If you cannot get a dial tone on any phone in the house, unplug them all. Plug them back in, one at a time, and listen to each. One phone may cause all your phones to go dead. You can find it by the process of elimination and have it repaired.

If you are plagued with wrong numbers when you dial out with a rotary dial phone, the dial may be returning too slowly after you release it. The dial may need replacing or the hook-shaped dial-stop, into which you run your finger, may be rubbing against the dial, slowing its return. If so, bend it so it clears the dial. Check your dialing habits, too. You may be "helping" the dial back. Forcing the dial back can cause the phone to dial incorrect numbers.

Diagnose the Telephone Problem

Let's say you pick up the telephone in the bedroom and it doesn't seem to work properly. If you can make a call but there is static on the line, try banging the handset on the table. That sometimes clears up the difficulty by loosening the carbon granules in the mouthpiece. Unfortunately, the get-a-bigger-hammer school of telephone repair is not often effective. Static can also be caused by worn cords. Shake the cords while listening to the phone. If the static seems related to the movements, replace the cords.

If your bedroom phone won't work at all, try another phone in the house to see if it works. If it does, plug that working phone into the jack in the bedroom. If the second phone still works well, the problem is almost certainly in the original phone. But what if you have only one telephone? Borrow a phone from a neighbor, bring it home and plug it in. If the borrowed phone works, then it's likely your trouble is in your own phone. If you don't feel right about borrowing a phone from your neighbor, take the telephone over to the neighbor's and plug it in there to test it.

TABLE 6
AT&T Repair Charges

Here is what it will cost you to have AT&T repair your AT&T telephone and work on the wires in your house. Your local telephone company will also work on your wiring (often at rates below AT&T's), but it usually won't fix telephone instruments. Local repair companies are usually less costly. Call AT&T at 800-555-8111 with repair questions and to make arrangements for service.

• House call to repair old hard-wired phones owned by AT&T. $15 for first fifteen minutes (includes new modular phone and jack installed). Any other work on that call is billed at $15 per fifteen minutes.

• House call to repair modular phones owned by AT&T. $25 for first fifteen minutes. Any other work on that call is $15 per fifteen minutes.

• House call to repair home wiring. $25 for first fifteen minutes, $15 per fifteen minutes thereafter. Local phone companies often charge less to do the same work.

• Repair rotary dial AT&T phone you own at AT&T phone center. $12.50 to fix the works, $14 for new case, $18 to do both, plus $6 shipping (if necessary).

• Repair Touch-tone AT&T phone you own at AT&T phone center. $15 to fix the works, $15 for new case, $21 for both, plus $6 shipping, if necessary.

When one of your telephone instruments doesn't work, take a long look at the cords to the handset and to the wall jack before you start looking for a repair person. If either cord is frayed, you may be able to solve your problem by simply replacing one of them. When you go to the store to buy a new cord, take a look at all the different lengths of cords that are for sale. Maybe you'd like a longer one. If a cord is not the problem, try replacing the handset from a working phone. By swapping cords and handsets, you should be able to isolate the part that is not working.

If you still can't figure out what's wrong with your phone, you have some choices to make. If you paid $20 or less for the phone, walk directly to the nearest trash basket and, without ceremony, drop it in. It is almost certainly not worth fixing. Buy a new phone instead.

If you are still leasing your phones from AT&T, you can take your broken phone to an AT&T Phone Center or AT&T service agency, turn it in, and get another. AT&T will give you a new phone (or a refurbished phone with a new cover), no questions asked. You can get a new phone for any reason—even if it's only that one is dirty.

If you live a long distance from an AT&T store—or you don't know where one might be in your neighborhood—call 800-555-8111 (twenty-four hours a day), and a person from AT&T in Jacksonville will help you. If there isn't an AT&T store nearby, AT&T will send you another phone by one of the commercial delivery services and pick up your broken phone. If your phone is so old that it is wired to the wall, be sure to tell the AT&T person. He or she will tell you to cut the wire to the old phone. Along with a new phone that requires a modular jack, AT&T will send a new modular jack and directions on how to install it. Since you have read Chapter 5, of course, you'll already know how to do that.

If you believe your time is worth more than your money and you want a real repair person to take care of your problem, AT&T will still come out to your house to fix a phone that you lease from the company. (If you own your own telephone, AT&T will not make a service call to fix it, even if you bought it from AT&T.)

To summon the AT&T repair person, call AT&T at 800-555-

8111. Don't expect AT&T to make the trip for free, however. If you are still leasing, and your phone is hard-wired to the wall outlet, the charge for the house call is $15. During the call, the repair person will put in a modular jack for the broken phone and give you a new modular phone. He'll do any other repair or phone installation work—such as putting in an extension phone—for $15 every fifteen minutes. If you already have modular jacks, and the repair person doesn't have to install one, the charge for the call is $25. Wait a minute, you say, it costs more to have the repair person simply swap a leased phone than it does to have him swap a phone *and* install an outlet? Right. AT&T wants to discourage owners of modular phones from calling for service on modular phones. They want you to take the phone in for repairs.

Some AT&T Phone Centers have facilities for fixing phones you own on the spot; others do not. If you take your phone to a Center that does not do repairs, it will cost you $6 to have the store send it off to where it can be fixed. If you call 800-555-8111 and get an address where you can send your phone, it will cost only about $4.50 to mail the phone. AT&T's repair costs are flat-rate: $15 to fix the insides of a touch-tone phone, $15 to fix the outside (the case), or $21 to do both at the same time. To do the same for a rotary dial phone is $12.50 to fix the works, $14 to change the outside case, or $18 to do both.

Just because you own your AT&T-manufactured phones doesn't mean AT&T is the only company that can fix it. A growing number of telephone stores offer repair services for AT&T and most other popular brands of telephones. Since many telephone repairs ought to cost $10 to $20, you can probably save money at a local repair shop. They may offer you a loaner while yours is being fixed. Look in the Yellow Pages under "Telephone Equipment & Systems-Dealers." If the store you call doesn't repair phones, ask for their recommendations about repair shops.

Trouble on the Lines

What if you find that all your telephone instruments work perfectly, but you can't make or receive calls? That probably means the trouble is somewhere in the wires, either those in your residence or somewhere in the local phone company's network. Take your good telephone to the point where the phone line comes into the house. There, if you have had work done on your phones recently, you'll find a network interface jack. It's a regular modular jack that was installed by the phone company near the station protector. (See Chapter 4.) All your house wiring is plugged into that network interface jack.

Unplug your house wiring from the network interface jack. Plug a phone that you know works into the NIJ. If you don't have an NIJ, use the modular jack that is closest to the point where the telephone company's line comes in. If you can make a call and the phone system operates well, you have isolated the problem. It's somewhere in your house wiring.

But if you can't make your good phone work at the network interface jack, you can be fairly certain the trouble is in the phone company's system. Now you can call them to complain without the worry that you will be socked with a big service call fee. It's *their* problem.

If you find that the phone works when you plug it into the network interface jack but it doesn't when you plug it in elsewhere in your house, you know the problem is somewhere in the phone wires in your walls. That is very unusual, but not impossible. Before you start looking for the trouble, check your phone bill or call the local phone company to see if you are paying a monthly fee—usually about fifty cents—to have the local phone company maintain your inside wires. If you are paying the fee, call the phone company and they'll come for nothing.

The "optional inside wiring maintenance plan," as our local phone company calls it, was offered when the Bell System was broken up. If you returned a post card saying you did not want the wiring maintenance plan, your phone bill went down fifty cents a month and you became responsible for your own wiring. Since it's always easier to do nothing than to do something, most people opted to pay the fifty cents a month. But when was the last time you heard of the wires in a friend's house failing? Given the odds of an inside-wire problem developing, you'd be well-advised to pass up this insurance. Ten years at fifty cents a month is $60, not counting interest. It's highly unlikely you'd have a wiring mishap every ten years—and if you did, the cost to fix it would probably be less than $60, even if you paid the phone company to come out.

When dealing with your phone, it's a good idea never to say never, however, and that applies to inside wiring. If you can't make or receive calls and you've determined that your telephone instruments themselves work, and they work at the network interface jack, your inside wiring is probably at fault.

Begin your search for trouble where work—in your house or your phone system—was last done. A carpenter—you, perhaps—may have hammered a nail through a phone cable, shorting it. An over-enthusiastic plumber may have blowtorched a modular jack. Trace the phone line wherever you can, inspecting it. You may find a simple answer at the remodeling job-site. If you installed the wire yourself, look at places where you cheated and spliced the cable. Replace the splice with a terminal block or wire junction.

If you can't find a solution at the last place where work was done, examine all your terminal blocks, modular jacks, and junction boxes. Check all screws to make sure they are snug—and that the phone wires are securely under them as they should be. If you find water in a jack, eliminate the cause or, if necessary, relocate the jack.

Fixing the Wiring Problem

Nearly all wiring problems—exclusive of jacks, terminal blocks, and junction boxes—are caused by shorted or crossed wires, bare wires touching a grounded conductor (like a water pipe) or a break in a wire. You have to find the short, the spot where a wire is grounded, or the break.

Rig a test apparatus out of a short telephone cord with a modular plug at one end, two alligator clips, and a double-jack cord-extender (a little piece of plastic, the size of a thimble, with a jack at each end). Alligator clips, available at any electronics store, have jaws that look like those of an alligator. Squeeze the clips and the spring-loaded jaws open; release, and they clamp solidly to things like screws in telephone blocks. Wire one alligator clip to the red wire of the cable with the modular plug and the other to the green wire. Stick the modular plug into one jack of the cord-extender and a working telephone into the other. Now you have a phone that has two alligator clips at the end of its cord. You are prepared to start looking for trouble.

Go to the network interface jack. A short distance away you should find a wire junction. A cord from the wire junction is plugged into the network interface jack. The house telephone wires lead from the wire junction. Disconnect all the wires from the wire junction, taking care to remember where each came from. It is a good idea to tape a piece of paper to each wire to note where it was attached. Once you have all the wires disconnected, check your new test apparatus to see that it is working. Fasten red wire alligator clip to red wire screw on the wire junction. Fasten green wire alligator clip to green wire screw. Now when you lift the receiver on your test phone you should get a dial tone and be able to make a call.

Reconnect one pair of wires to the junction. Check to see if the phones on that circuit are working. If they are, you know that circuit is good. Connect the wires, one pair at a time, till you find the pair that is not working. When you find the one wire that is not working correctly, follow it to its end. Work from the network interface jack to the end of the circuit. Every time you come to a wire junction, a modular jack, or a terminal block, disconnect the wires. Get out your new test phone assembly, clip the alligators to the red and green wires, and listen for a dial tone. If you can make a call, you know the trouble is farther upstream. Rewire the jack and go to the next step. Finally, after moving up the circuit step by step, you should be able to isolate the section of wire that has the fault. Then you must either find the fault and fix it—or lay a new wire to replace the one with the problem.

Sometimes there is nothing wrong with your phone except that it looks old and dirty. You can clean a telephone, but you should be careful. Wipe it with a damp—not sopping wet—sponge. If that won't take off the accumulated grime, use a little soap on the sponge. Be careful around the keypad or rotary dial, and don't let water drip into the receiver. You can remove the cords and wash them in soap and water as long as the modular plugs are dry before you plug them in again.

In a fit of complusiveness, one of us once took a soapy sponge to a filthy office phone. The phone came out clean and shiny—and dead as a doornail. We had soaked the keypad. Sheepishly, we called the telephone company to say their phone was broken. That was bad enough. By the time the friendly telephone repair person showed up a few hours later, the keypad had dried out and was working perfectly.

3

How to Save on Telephone Services

CHAPTER 8 Choosing the Best Local Service Plan

A revolution is not a dinner party, a famous Chinese revolutionary once observed, and in the context of the telephone revolution, we're afraid that means local rate increases that should send local telephone bills substantially higher all around. The only way to mitigate the effect on your pocketbook is to assure that you have chosen the proper local service alternative. This chapter describes the most common options available from the local telephone company and explains how to determine which one best suits your calling habits. Our purpose here is to show you how to avoid paying more than is absolutely necessary for local telephone service.

A revolution is a revolution, however, and whatever you do to control the damage, it is inevitable that local telephone prices will rise significantly in the next few years. In many states the process is already well under way. Wisconsin and Virginia residents saw their phone rates for unrestricted local service increase by more than 35 percent since the start of 1984, and in a number of other states there are rate requests that would more than double local calling charges. To compound the problem, the Federal Communications Commission has imposed an additional charge on residential subscribers to help maintain the national telephone network. As a result of this levy, which is called a "subscriber line charge," or "access charge," residential customers will pay an additional $1 per month to their local phone company, beginning in June of 1985. The charge is to rise to $2 per month in June of 1986, and is likely to be supplemented by similar "taxes" ordered by state regulatory authorities. When combined with the huge increases in the cost of telephone installation and repairs, residential phone service is becoming a significant expense for many American households.

Because the runup of local rates coincides wtih the dismantling of AT&T, it's natural to want to blame Ma Bell's breakup for the escalation in local rates. But in this case, AT&T is being held guilty by association. The real impetus to raise rates came from a series of complicated decisions by the FCC in the late 1970s and early 1980s to rearrange the way local telephone companies were paid for providing local phone service. While AT&T aided and abetted some of these decisions, technological change and the introduction of competition to the industry made the FCC's course of action almost inevitable. By the time the decision was made to undo Ma Bell, the genie was long out of the bottle.

Before you curse the FCC, the genie, or what the current occupant of the White House likes to call "the magic of the marketplace," you should know that one of the major consequences of this revolution is lower long-distance phone prices for everyone. We'll tell you how to take advantage of these dividends in the next two chapters. But before we look at long-distance, let us examine how to limit the financial pain from local rate increases.

Flat vs. Measured Service

The first question in selecting local service is whether to choose a flat-rate or measured service plan. Under a flat-rate option, you pay a fixed monthly rate, which entitles you to make unlimited local calls at no additional expense.

Measured-service plans carry lower monthly fees, but require additional charges based on the number of calls you make and how long these calls last. In the telephone business, this is called "usage-sensitive" pricing.

The choice you make will depend on what your local calling patterns are. While you may think you know how much you use the phone locally, you'd be surprised how few people really know their calling habits. One way to check yourself is to keep a log of all your local calls for a week or two. We've included a sample log below for your use.

_____ TABLE 7 _____
Log of Outgoing Local and Long-distance Calls

	LOCAL			LONG DISTANCE		
Date	# Called	Time Elapsed	# Called	Time of Day	Day of Week	Time Elapsed

The higher the number of local calls you make, the more likely a flat-rate plan will benefit you. But different states have different rates for local service, and the point at which a flat-rate option is cost-effective will differ from state to state. The arithmetic will look quite different in Illinois, where flat-rate service costs over $30 a month, than in California, where the option is just over $8 a month.

To pick the best plan, you will not only need to know the price of flat-rate service in your state, but how the cost of measured service compares, given your local calling habits. Millions of people forget to do this comparison and pay dearly. Even in California, which has among the lowest flat-rate charges in the country, the local telephone company contends that 60 percent of its customers would save money by switching from flat to measured service.

Most local telephone companies have a fee for switching from one rate plan to another. In some places it can be more than $25. But if you've chosen well, you'll usually be able to pay back that fee in savings within a year at most.

Types of Measured Service

Flat-rate plans offer the subscriber one rate and no more. Within the measured-service category, customers will usually have at least a couple of options from which to choose. While the names of these options may differ from state to state, there are several generic types.

Economy Service

Also known as Budget Service, this option usually provides for a low monthly service fee ($3-$6) and additional usage charges for every local call that's made. The usage charges are figured either on a "message unit" or on a per-call basis. In some jurisdictions, message units are synonymous with the number of calls made. In other states, they are calibrated to factor in time of day, day of the week, and calling distance and duration for purposes of billing. Economy Service is for consumers who want to keep their local phone costs down, and don't mind paying as they go. While the option is geared to the needs of low-income consumers, many frugal but affluent subscribers use it to cut the costs of maintaining a phone at a vacation home or other infrequently used location. Some even subscribe to Budget Service for their primary residence because they do most of their calling at their offices during the day.

Standard Measured Service

The monthly service fee for Standard Measured Service is several dollars more than the Economy Service, but there is a fairly generous message unit allowance before the customer must begin to pay any usage-sensitive charges. Instead of calculating the allowance in message units, some states define the allowance in terms of the number or dollar-value of calls that can be made without incurring usage-sensitive charges. Standard Measured Service is for the customer who makes enough local calls to be able to take advantage of the option's call allowance, but doesn't do enough calling to justify a flat-rate option.

Exchange-Only Unlimited Service

A cross between flat and measured service, the Exchange-Only plan allows unlimited service within your immediate exchange for a flat monthly rate that is in the same range as Standard Measured Service. Local calls beyond the exchange are billed by message units, with no call allowance provided. This is an attractive option if most of your calls fall within your exchange. (Calls to phones within your exchange have the same first three digits as your number.)

Lifeline Service

With the sharp climb in local phone rates of all types, there is a concern in many quarters that local telephone service is becoming too expensive for low-income groups to afford. To ease the threat, governmental entities at the federal and the state levels have been examining ways to help low-income individuals bear the burden of local phone rate increases. Several state legislatures and public utility commissions have established a "Lifeline" service option for financially disadvantaged consumers.

Under the Lifeline option, individuals below a certain income level qualify to receive service at a single monthly rate subsidized by state taxes on long-distance companies doing business within their boundaries. Because of the subsidy, the Lifeline rate can be

as little as half the monthly cost of Economy Service in participat-
ing states. The Lifeline option normally entitles subscribers to
twenty or thirty local calls a month without further charge. Once
the call allowance is exceeded, the subscriber must pay for additional calls on a per-call basis.

In California, which has been a Lifeline service pioneer, a
subscriber's income must not exceed $11,000 to qualify for the
option. Customers meeting the income test pay $1.48 a month for
the service, and are allowed thirty local calls at no additional
expense. For calls numbering thirty-one through forty, there's a
ten-cent-per-call charge. Anything beyond costs fifteen cents a
call. To subsidize California's extremely low Lifeline rate, the state
legislature imposed a special 4 percent state tax on revenues that
long-distance carriers collected from their customers within the
state.

The Higher Costs of Staying in Touch and Informed

As part of their campaign to raise their rates wherever they can,
most local telephone companies already have or are planning to
raise their charge for using a pay telephone. In many states it now
costs a quarter to make a pay call.

Local phone companies have also begun to charge customers for
providing directory assistance information. Generally they allow
ten or so free information requests a month, then begin charging
fifteen to twenty cents per additional call. To limit your directory
assistance expenses, get in the habit of writing down numbers you
call frequently. If you need two numbers, ask for both of them at
the same time—once you call directory assistance, there's no
charge for a second listing. When the party you are calling has
recently moved, before going to directory assistance, try calling
the old number to see if there is a recording that gives the new
number. To obtain phone books for both surrounding and far-off
areas, call your local business office during working hours. A

White Pages for Manhattan would cost you $8.55 and a Yellow Pages, $8.15, for instance. If you must look up numbers from those areas frequently, ordering your own books might be a good investment.

Subscriber Line Charges and the Bypass Threat

As if the rise in local phone rates isn't bad enough, your friends at the Federal Communications Commission have invented yet another way to tap your pocketbook—subscriber line charges.

Subscriber line charges are a concept first developed by the FCC to provide added financial support to the local telephone companies through the imposition of special monthly surcharges on both residential and business telephone subscribers. Under a plan imposed by the FCC in 1984, residential customers must now pay an extra $1 per month per line for local service, beginning in June of 1985. That fee is to rise to $2 per month per line beginning in June of 1986. In addition, the FCC has left the door open for state regulatory authorities to increase these fees to the local phone companies by another thirty-five cents per month. For businesses with more than one line, there are now subscriber line charges of as much as $6 per month per line. Some low-income households may be exempted from the charges levied by the FCC, but for most subscribers, they mean higher monthly local phone bills. To make matters worse, a number of states are considering, or have imposed, access charges of their own for intrastate services.

The FCC rationalizes subscriber line charges by explaining that when you ask your local telephone company for service, you receive an important additional benefit, which is the capability of using the local telephone network to make and receive long-distance calls. It is only fair, the Commission argues, that you should make a contribution to the local telephone company for this "access" to the long-distance system, as well.

This may sound like a lot of fast talking, designed to make you pay for something that always has been free before. But according to the FCC, you've always paid this freight in the past; the means of collecting it has just been more indirect.

From the day commercial telephone service began in Boston in 1877, the biggest expense of providing service has come from the poles and wires that connect your home with the local telephone office. Since there could be no phone system without these lines, the costs of installing and maintaining this network existed whether anyone used his phone or not. None of the technological wizardry of the last century has ever been able to change that.

As long as phone service was confined to a local area, the local phone companies had no choice but to accept their high, fixed costs as the price of doing business. All this changed with the spread of interstate long-distance service in the early part of this century. Since all long-distance calls had to travel over the local phone companies' lines, the local operating companies argued that part of their enormous fixed expense should be paid out of long-distance revenues. To AT&T, this was just an accounting measure, in part, because it not only owned the vast majority of local telephone companies, but controlled the entire long-distance business, as well. The amount of fixed expense allocated to the long-distance side of AT&T's business was small at first, but by the late 1970s, about half the revenue from long-distance service was being passed along to the local operating companies.

Whether AT&T's long-distance arm was really "subsidizing" rates or just paying its fair share of the fixed costs of maintaining the local network, is a question of sharp theological dispute within the industry. What is indisputable is that the contributions from long-distance service kept local rates much lower than they otherwise would have been. At the same time, your long-distance bills were probably kept higher than they needed to be to help defray some of AT&T's contribution to the fixed cost of the local operating companies.

For reasons that need not concern us here, the dawning of telecommunications competition in the 1970s and the appearance of companies like MCI made the death of the old system, in which AT&T "settled up" with its operating subsidiaries, inevitable. But the FCC couldn't just junk the old method without providing some way for the local operating companies to replace the enormous contributions on which they had come to rely from AT&T. Its answer was subscriber line charges.

As residential customers, there's nothing you can do about subscriber line charges. Since they're designed to apply to anyone with a phone, regardless of calling patterns, you can't adjust your calling habits to avoid them. Fortunately, even at the $2-per-month level in 1986, the residential subscriber line charges aren't likely to spell your financial downfall.

Telephone industry experts argue that without subscriber line charges to help local telephone companies keep their rates down, the financial underpinnings of their business will be undermined by a phenomenon known as telephone "bypass." Bypass occurs when telephone subscribers, particularly corporate ones, conclude that they can satisfy their long-distance needs more cheaply by constructing a private communications system at their office that enables them to leapfrog the local phone system when placing long-distance calls. Business bypass is of vital concern because a disproportionate amount of the local operating companies' revenue base comes from business, rather than residential, customers. Of the revenue generated from business customers, a very high percentage is derived from a handful of major companies. To the extent that subscriber line charges raise businesses' costs in using the local phone network and encourage bypass by major business customers, the financial impact on local telephone companies could be devastating.

Even without FCC-imposed subscriber line charges of as much as $6 a month for multi-line businesses, Pacific Bell reports that 30 percent of its revenue in California comes from less than 1 percent of its business customers. Of these large business customers, half are either working on bypass plans or have begun bypassing already, claims the telephone company. Once the trend to bypass starts, local telephone companies can be exposed to a double jeopardy of sorts, because the more they raise their rates to compensate for loss of revenue to bypass, the more bypass they are likely to provoke.

The danger, suggests Massachusetts Congressman Edward Markey, is that we'll develop a "communications aristocracy" and a "communications underclass" in this country because of bypass.

Those with means will leave the public system to construct superior private facilities to meet their needs, while those with fewer resources will be stuck with a deteriorating public network. Fortunately, for many of us, lower costs for equipment and long-distance calling should be enough to offset the effects of higher local rates.

CHAPTER 9
What Has Happened to Long-distance?

In the Fall of 1984, 93 million Americans went to the polls to elect a new president. The issues were war and peace, megadeficits, the size of government, and the restoration of our national spirit. Sometime in 1985 and 1986, you will all be asked to vote again. While the ballot question won't be quite as cosmic this time, the day-to-day impact on you may be just as great. Under the terms of the breakup of Ma Bell, seven out of ten American households will be able to designate a long-distance telephone company to handle the bulk of their long-distance calling by the end of 1986.

This courting of the hearts and minds of long-distance customers is known as the "equal access" process. The objectives of the process are twofold: One is to put all of AT&T's competitors in the long-distance field on a "level playing field" with AT&T as to the technical quality of their connections from the local telephone companies to originate and conclude long-distance calls. The other is to make it as easy for consumers to use one of AT&T's long-distance competitors as it is to call on AT&T. As a result of the process, consumers will be given the opportunity to choose among the long-distance companies oper-

ating in their market a "primary carrier" for their long-distance
calling.

Just as in the political arena, where candidates use the air-
waves and local newspapers, telephone solicitations, neighborhood leafletting campaigns, and even door-to-door canvassing
to woo voters during election season, the scores of companies
now competing with AT&T in providing long-distance telephone
service are leaving no marketing tools untried in their fight for
your long-distance affections over the next two years. In
Charleston, West Virginia, which was called the "New Hampshire primary" of this campaign when it became the first city in
the United States to face equal access in the summer of 1984,
families had to turn off their telephones at mealtime to escape
the calls of salesmen hawking long-distance services. Some
Charleston small business owners complained that there were
so many "account reps" in their offices during the campaign
that at times it became difficult to turn around. One long-
distance company executive went so far as to describe his
company's blitz in Charleston as the "Rolling Thunder" campaign.

While there's been competition in the long-distance field since
the mid-1970s, prior to equal access customers had to have a
touch-tone telephone and dial as many as fourteen extra digits in
order to use a long-distance company other than AT&T. This
was to compensate for the fact that the kind of connections the
local phone companies provided the alternative carriers required extra switching to place a call. The only way to do that
switching was by using a touch-tone phone to dial added digits.
Even so, calls made on an alternative carrier often had an echo,
or sounded "fuzzy" because of the extra switching involved in
getting through. Since 50 percent of the country's phones are
still rotary-dial rather than touch-tone-dial, that meant that half
of the nation's telephone subscribers were unable to take advantage of discount phone services before equal access.

Equal access makes the alternative carriers as easy to use as
AT&T. To place your call on an alternative carrier, your dialing
will be exactly the same as it is now on AT&T. In communities
where you must now dial "1" to originate a long-distance call,
you will dial 1 + the area code + the local number you wish to

reach to complete your call. If you live in an area where the "1" is not required to call long distance, all you'll have to do is dial an area code + local number to make your call. It will make no difference whether your phone is touch-tone or rotary.

Once you receive equal access, many discrepancies in the quality of the alternative carriers and AT&T ought to also disappear. If differences continue, it will be because some long-distance carriers' networks are better than others. It will no longer have anything to do with the kind of connections that local telephone companies provide. For better or worse, equal access also should enable alternative carriers to be much more accurate in billing you.

Because of the technical requirements in converting to equal access, the process can generally only be accomplished telephone exchange by telephone exchange. (An exchange is the local switch represented by the first three numerals in your local telephone number.) This means that not everyone in the same town or even neighborhood will get equal access at the same time. The more modern your area's switching equipment, the earlier your local telephone exchange is likely to be converted.

During 1985, between ten to fifteen major communities a week will be "cutting over" to equal access, in the lingo of the telephone industry. You'll find a list of the cities where cutovers will be occurring in Table 9 at the conclusion of this chapter. By the end of the year, about 40 million American households will have crossed the equal access bridge. By the end of 1986, it's estimated that another 25 million families will have joined them.

The scenario by which consumers must select a "primary carrier" for their long-distance calling is called the "presubscription" process. Presubscription refers to the fact that you will be asked to choose a primary carrier from among the companies operating in your area *before* the actual implementation of equal access. Here's how the process is to work: Ninety days before equal access goes into effect in your community, your local telephone company will notify you by mail of your coming choice and include a list of the long-distance companies serving your area.

There may be as few as three companies and as many as thirty to choose from, depending on the market. The list will always include AT&T Communications, which is the name of the AT&T division offering long-distance service. Other companies likely to be involved include MCI, GTE Sprint, ITT, Western Union, and Satellite Business Systems, which is a partnership of IBM and Aetna Insurance Company. Known by the industry as "other common carriers," or OCCs for short, these carriers own at least some of their own switching facilities and operate nationwide.

In addition to the OCCs, there will probably be several other companies known as "resellers" in your market. Resellers are carriers that own few, if any, of their own facilities. Instead, they merely buy transmission time wholesale from carriers with nationwide service such as AT&T or MCI, and resell it to customers at a retail markup. Because the capital investment of entering the long-distance market as a reseller is very low, there are hundreds of these carriers operating today. A handful of these companies, such as Chicago-based Allnet and U.S. Telephone, which calls its residential service Homeline II, operate in dozens of (but not all) markets across the country. Most resellers serve only a region, and some originate calls from only one or two cities. When two relatively wealthy ladies from California got tired of being ranchers, for instance, they put up $350,000 to buy a switch, leased space on some long-distance lines, and before they knew it, they were in business.

Along with the list of carriers in your area, you will receive a form on which to specify which company you wish to designate as your primary carrier. You are to mark this form and return it to your local phone company so that it knows which carrier to assign your long-distance traffic. As an alternative, you may also contact the long-distance company of your choice directly to subscribe, and ask that carrier to make whatever arrangements are necessary with your local telephone company, on your behalf. Frequently, the carriers will initiate the contact with you, and if you decide to subscribe to one, all you have to do is take the form provided to you by the long-distance carrier and mail it to your local phone company.

You have three months before equal access is in place, and six months after, in which to designate a primary carrier without being charged. If you wait longer than that, or if you wish to change your selection after you have made an initial choice, there is a $5 service charge that is paid to the local telephone company. It's unlikely that you'll ever be charged for switching, however. To win your business, many of the carriers are willing to pick up that $5 charge for you if you switch to them.

Any time you move, you have a month to specify a primary carrier at your new location, free of charge. The company providing long-distance at your old address will not automatically serve your new one. If you don't select a new primary carrier within a month of moving, you must pay the same $5 fee that is required for switching primary carriers.

If you do not choose a carrier by the time equal access is implemented, or within a month of moving, most of the local telephone companies will route your long-distance calls to AT&T by default. This could occur even if you have previously been using one of the alternative long-distance services. The only phone company that is not currently defaulting undirected calls to AT&T is US West, which serves fourteen Western states. In the interest of fairness, US West is allocating undirected calls between competing carriers on a formula determined by the relative market shares of the various carriers in its territory. The FCC is considering encouraging other local telephone companies to follow a similar approach to insure that AT&T does not keep the lion's share of the long-distance market by default.

Old habits die hard, we know, and we can understand if you're a little nervous about moving from tried-and-true AT&T to one of the Johnny-come-lately long-distance carriers. But the equal access process is not like marriage, and your selection of a primary carrier comes with no obligation to be monogamous. While you will be able to reach your primary long-distance carrier just by dialing 1 (where required) + the area code + local number you are calling, there is a simple backup dialing procedure that enables you to make calls on any of the other carriers operating in your area, should you wish. All you have to do is dial "1" + "0" + a three-digit company code for the carrier you want to use before dialing the area code and local number of the party you are calling. This backup option allows you to direct your traffic to a company other than your primary

carrier when an alternative carrier is offering a better rate to the
city you wish to call. We have listed the special backup access
codes for some of the leading long-distance companies in Table 8
below.

--------------------------------- TABLE 8 ---------------------------------
If You Want to Use Another Carrier

Company	Five-Digit Access Code
ALLNET	10444
ATT	10288
GTE/SPRINT	10777
ITT	10488
MCI	10222
SBS	10888
WESTERN UNION	10220

You can't have dominated the long-distance business for a
hundred years without having some advantages over new competitors, and AT&T still claims a few. As that celebrated industry expert, Cliff Robertson, points out in his commercials for
AT&T, his sponsor is the only carrier that has its own long-
distance operators on the line, should you need to place a call
person-to-person or collect (although at least one other company, MCI, is considering the option). It is also the only
company that can offer you full, international long-distance
service. Several other carriers, notably MCI and Sprint, are
developing international service, but if you need to call spots
from Andorra to Zimbabwe, AT&T is still the only game in
town.

Before you make too big a deal of these points, there are
several things you should keep in mind, however. While it is
currently true that only AT&T has operators to handle collect
and person-to-person calls, several of the alternative carriers
should have this capability before long. Meanwhile, the equal-
access system gives you the option of using AT&T for operator-

assisted calls, even if it is not your primary carrier. All you have to do is dial AT&T's five-digit access code (see Table 8) and then ring the operator. Don't expect these services to come cheaply, however. The last time we looked, there was a $1.55 surcharge for calling collect or billing a long-distance call to a third number, and a service charge of $3.00 for a person-to-person call.

Long-distance directory assistance will still be available, but not for free. After years of receiving the service free of charge, AT&T customers must now pay fifty cents per call after a monthly allowance of two free calls. A number of AT&T's competitors are providing the service for forty-five cents per call once their monthly two-call allowance is exceeded. If your primary carrier doesn't offer long-distance directory assistance, you're free to use AT&T's service if you pay. Just dial AT&T's five-digit backup code, followed by an area code + 555-1212. The backup system for completing international long-distance calls is much the same as for operator and directory assistance. If the carrier you are using doesn't serve the country you wish to call, you have only to dial AT&T's five-digit access code and place your call on AT&T. The amount of extra dialing required to use AT&T on a backup basis for international calls is trivial. Unless you're a heavy international caller, we'd advise you simply to ignore the question of international service in choosing a primary long-distance carrier.

Confusing as all this change may sound, equal access should work to your ultimate benefit as a consumer. While there were many alternative long-distance carriers that could save you money before equal access, almost none of them could make the kind of technical connections to the local network that would have enabled them to offer quality as good as AT&T's. Equal access changes all that. For the first time, the alternative long-distance carriers are in a position to compete with AT&T on quality as well as on price. To compensate for losing the edge it always held on quality, AT&T will almost certainly have to be more aggressive in competing with the discount carriers on price. The winner in this competition should be you.

TABLE 9
When Will I Get Equal Access?

The schedule of conversions to equal access in 1985 is still being compiled. Here's the latest information on cutovers in major cities. Some cities may be listed more than once, because only one or two switches are being converted at one time.

CUTOVER DATE	CITY, STATE
Jan. 1, 1985	LaPuente, CA; Santa Monica, CA; Long Beach, CA; Westminster, CA
Jan. 5	Roberts, WI; Houlton, WI; Hudson, WI; Janesville, WI
Jan. 6	Richmond, VA; Washington, DC; Somerville, NJ
Jan. 11	Visalia, CA
Jan. 12	Dayton, OH; South Bend, IN; Hudson, NH; Manchester, NH; Nashua, NH
Jan. 14	Miami, FL; Memphis, TN
Jan. 18	San Jose, CA
Jan. 19	Buffalo, NY; some NYC offices
Jan. 20	Boise, ID
Jan. 21	Birmingham, AL
Jan. 25	San Diego, CA; Chicago, IL
Jan. 26	Dayton, OH; Oklahoma City, OK; Springfield, MO; Kansas City, KS; Wichita, KS
Jan. 27	Midland, El Paso, TX
Jan. 28	Orlando, FL; Savannah, GA; Baton Rouge, LA; Chattanooga, Memphis, TN; Nashville, TN; W. Louisville, KY
Feb. 1	Los Angeles, CA
Feb. 2	Staten Island, NY; Ft. Worth, San Antonio, TX; Milwaukee, WI
Feb. 3	Tucson, AZ; Albuquerque, NM; Cincinnati, OH; Philadelphia, Pittsburgh, PA
Feb. 4	Orlando, FL; Charlotte, NC
Feb. 8	Sacramento, CA
Feb. 9	Kansas City, St. Louis, MO; Tulsa, OK
Feb. 11	Atlanta, GA; Shreveport, LA
Feb. 16	Detroit, Ann Arbor, MI; Wellesley, MA

CUTOVER DATE	CITY, STATE
Feb. 22	San Bruno, Fullerton, CA
Feb. 23	Syracuse, NY; Houston, Ft. Worth, TX; Toledo, OH
Feb. 24	Phoenix, AZ
Feb. 25	Miami, Palm Beach, FL; Atlanta, Augusta, GA; Birmingham, AL; Louisville, KY; Knoxville, TN
March 1	Sunnyvale, Sacramento, CA
March 2	Dallas, TX; Bronx, some NYC, White Plains, NY
March 3	Harrisburg, PA; Passaic, NJ; Bethesda, MD
March 6	Minneapolis, MN
March 8	Los Angeles, Sacramento, CA
March 9	Houston, TX; Boston, MA
March 13	El Paso, TX; Minneapolis, MN
March 15	Omaha, NE
March 16	Tulsa, OK; Houston, TX; Framingham, MA; Grand Rapids, MI; New York, NY
March 23	Queens, NY; Pittsfield, MA; Little Rock, AR; Houston, TX
March 25	Ft. Lauderdale, Miami, FL; Memphis, TN; New Orleans, LA
March 26	St. Paul, MN
March 29	Indianapolis, IN; San Antonio, TX
March 30	Cleveland, OH; Dallas, TX; Oklahoma City, OK; Detroit, MI; Buffalo, Brooklyn, NY
March 31	Des Moines, IA
April 6	Long Beach, Stockton, CA; St. Louis, MO; Houston, TX; Cranston, RI
April 13	Lansing, MI; Little Rock, AR; Brookline, MA
April 19	Chicago, Hinsdale, Homewood, IL
April 20	NYC; Cambridge, Quincy, MA; Columbus, Dayton, OH
April 24	Minneapolis, MN
April 27	Del Mar, CA; Little Rock, AR; St. Louis, MO; Dallas, TX; Providence, RI
April 28	Denver, CO; Albuquerque, NM
May 1	Toledo, Zanesville, OH; Portland, OR; Seattle, WA

CUTOVER DATE	CITY, STATE
May 4	Flint, MI; New York, Brooklyn, Queens, NY; Newport, RI; Boston, Springfield, MA; Omaha, NE; Minneapolis, MN
May 15	Omaha, NE; Minneapolis, MN
May 18	Cleveland, OH; Battle Creek, MI; Albany, NY; Burlington, VT
May 25	Pawtucket, RI; Syracuse, NY
June 1	Albany, New York City, NY; Dorchester, MA; Salem, NH; Columbus, Akron, Canton, OH; Bronx, Brooklyn, NY; Vancouver, WA; Northbrook, IL
June 8	Portland, ME; Worcester, Dedham, MA
June 15	Lynn, Akron, OH; Omaha, NE; Des Moines, IA; Omaha, NE
June 22	Dearborn, Trenton, MI; New York City, Floral Park, NY; Waltham, MA
June 28	Chicago, IL
July 1	Milwaukee, WI

CHAPTER 10 Picking a Long-distance Company

In Chapter 2 we suggested that buying telephone equipment is like shopping for an automobile. You have to kick the tires, run the engine, and drive around the block before deciding that a car is for you. We hope we aren't overworking the metaphor by saying that selecting a primary long-distance carrier is like buying gas. One way to do it is to drive into the first gas station you see and tell the attendant to fill up your tank, regardless of price. That's the same as saying, "I can't be bothered with the equal access process. I'm sticking with AT&T, no matter what." Another way is to look at the prices at three or four nearby gas stations and choose among them. While this won't guarantee that you get absolutely the best value in town, it should insure that at least you get good value. A third way is to drive around for thirty miles, checking out the prices at twenty stations, selecting the very cheapest gas, and pumping it yourself. While your analytical decision may be right, you'll probably waste an hour and spill gas on your clothes.

It should be pretty clear to you what we suggest: from all the door knocking, letter writing, telephone calling, and media advertising that will be directed your way during the solicitation period for equal access in your community, pick out three or four carriers that seem at first glance to be capable of serving

"*Like Andy Griffith, you've recently had to make a most difficult decision regarding your telephone.*"

Drawing by Maslin; © 1984
The New Yorker Magazine, Inc.

your needs. You'll always want to include AT&T on this list. By virtue of its size and experience, it remains for better or worse the standard by which other carriers must be judged.

For other carriers, the threshold question is whether they serve the places you expect to call. MCI and GTE Sprint are the only two alternative carriers that can be said to be truly national in the range of locations from which they offer service today. These two carriers allow you to make calls, or "dial-up" their service, from almost four hundred cities, nationwide. The scope of other companies' operations vary greatly, with some "re-sale" carriers offering dial-up service from only one or two communities. The fact that a carrier only originates service in a few locations need not rule it out for you. Most plans today are able to complete calls to any location from the cities they serve. This capability is known as "universal termination."

Not all carriers offer universal termination, however. Some of the smaller resellers do not. Before you sign up with one of these carriers, you should be absolutely certain that you'll be able to call where you wish on that carrier.

Don't automatically dismiss resale carriers from your consideration. A number of them offer excellent value. But be aware that with over four hundred companies competing in the long-distance market today, there is bound to be a shakeout, and many of its victims are likely to come from the ranks of the small resellers.

As a second step, ask yourself, which companies' ads are clear and informative and address you in ways that respect your intelligence? Which companies' marketing efforts show some understanding of what's important to you as a consumer? Which companies' sales reps are knowledgeable enough to set aside canned sales pitches to listen and respond to questions you might have? Don't worry at this point whether you've chosen the very best three or four companies. The chances are 999 in 1000 that among the companies you've selected will be one or two that will be just fine for you.

Seek Good Quality at a Good Price

As anyone from Bucharest to Bismarck, North Dakota, knows, the more competitors in an industry, the more price competition there is. By this basic law of economics, long-distance telephone service should rival sex, jogging, and gossiping as one of the cheapest pastimes known to the American public. Trying to determine just how cheap, or how expensive, long-distance service is in the post-Bell world is often difficult, however, for the hundreds of long-distance companies in the field today all have different prices, depending on where you're calling from, what time of day you're talking, how long you're on the phone, what kind of transmission facilities you use, and how much calling you do each month.

The comrades of Bucharest and the citizenry of North Dakota will also tell you that telephone service can be as cheap as summer heat, but if you can't hear what's being said on the other end of the line, you might as well communicate with homing pigeons. If you believe in "nothing but the best, regardless of price" when it comes to telephone transmission quality, then you might well conclude that the service provided by some of the alternative carriers before equal access is, pardon the expression, for the birds.

A number of consumer information services have tried to sort out the price confusion by devising tables that would make it possible to compare different carriers' rates at a moment's glance. Several of these services have also done extensive "test calling" to assess the transmission quality of AT&T's competitors.

We wish we could give you such rate charts. We wish life fit nicely onto a 5 × 8 card. But as we discovered in trying to develop one of these tables ourselves, to represent even the major carriers' prices in a chart requires so many footnotes and caveats that meaningful comparisons become impossible. Even if we could develop a table that would allow for honest comparisons, prices change so quickly in this field that rate charts are outdated before they are completed.

Making black-and-white judgments about the adequacy of various carriers' transmission quality is also very problematic. For one thing, it's difficult for many callers to separate the issue of transmission quality from price. Even AT&T's competitors agree that until they get equal access to the local telephone network, there is no way their transmission quality can match AT&T's. Nevertheless, many customers are happy to accept the lower quality service and added digits that must be dialed as the trade-off for lower rates. What is more, the phasing in of equal access in 1985 and 1986 is likely to silence much of the present criticism about the transmission quality of the alternative carriers. If what the engineers promise us is right, there shouldn't be any appreciable difference in the transmission quality of the major carriers after equal access.

Rather than mislead you with price and service comparisons that mix apples with oranges and have the life expectancy of a mayfly, we'll spell out the kind of evaluation process you ought to follow to select a primary carrier, and suggest the kinds of questions to ask and considerations to weigh in your decision-making.

You're the Customer; Shop Accordingly

A cardinal rule in choosing carriers is to take ads and articles that compare a number of carriers' calling costs between a few selected city-pairs with a large pinch of salt. Rarely will the fact that carrier X is cheaper than competitors Y and Z between

Dubuque and Denver on the day the ad or article appears be a reliable indicator of whether you'll save money by using that carrier for the kinds of calls you make. When and where you call is a very personal matter, and unless cost comparisons are tailored to fit your calling patterns, they're not likely to be very illuminating to you.

The best way to make your market research match your needs is to analyze your calling habits by studying several of your past phone bills. When you have identified the types of calls you place most frequently, ask each of the carriers you are considering for rate information that will enable you to estimate what they'd charge you for such calling. In some cases the carrier may even provide the estimate directly. GTE Sprint has a "Personalized Rate Analysis" program, for instance, that provides potential customers with computer analyses of what they would save by using Sprint.

In areas where equal access campaigns are being waged, each company will probably have a local number to call for such information. Most of the major carriers will also have toll-free 800 numbers that you can call to get rate and other information or to sign up for their service. You will find a list of these numbers in Table 10 at the end of this chapter. When you reach a long-distance customer representative, here is what you need to know:

What Factors Are Used to Calculate the Price of a Long-distance Call?

When the equal access process began in 1984, over 90 percent of the interstate long-distance business still belonged to AT&T. As the dominant player in the field, AT&T naturally sets the pricing standard by which all other carriers must compete. AT&T's pricing system has *three* basic variables: how far you are calling, how long you talk, and at what time of day and day of the week you call. Calling distance is measured in mileage bands, with the smallest band covering calls from 1 to 10 miles and the largest band stretching from 4251 to 5750 miles. The bigger the mileage band, the more expensive your call.

Rates also fluctuate according to the length of call, with higher charges for the first minute of conversation than for subsequent minutes. The most expensive time to call is during weekday business hours, which is defined as Monday through Friday from 8 A.M. to 5 P.M. There are substantial discounts for calling during the evening period, which is defined as Sunday through Friday from 5 P.M. to 11 P.M., and during the night/weekend time-frame, which runs from 11 P.M. to 8 A.M. Sunday through Thursday, and from 11 P.M. Friday to 5 P.M. Sunday.

Recognizing that AT&T's pricing policies are, in Reggie Jackson's words, still "the straw that stirs the drink," a number of other carriers, including Allnet, GTE Sprint, ITT's "Longer-Distance" plan, and MCI have adopted AT&T's rate periods and mileage bands as their yardsticks for determining rates. The rates for these carriers are normally cheaper than AT&T's, but the way they are calculated is now the same.

Is There a Start-up Fee to Subscribe to a Particular Service?

None of the major carriers have start-up fees for residential service anymore, but a few of the lesser-known carriers catering to businesses do have sign-up charges. These fees can be over $100 in some cases.

Is There a Flat Monthly Fee?

A number of carriers charge monthly fees of $5 to $10, regardless of usage. The only national carrier that had such a charge at the end of 1984 was ITT, and even then, the charge only applied to ITT's Niteline service, which is designed for customers who only wish to call during non-business hours. If you are only an occa-sional long-distance caller, it probably won't make sense for you to choose a carrier with a flat monthly fee.

Is There a Minimum Monthly Usage Charge?

Several national carriers, including GTE Sprint, ITT Niteline, SBS, and Western Union impose minimum monthly usage require-ments on their customers. At the end of 1984, these monthly minimums ranged from $5 for GTE Sprint to $16 for ITT Niteline. For customers who fail to meet the minimums, the requirement works exactly the same as a flat monthly fee. You are billed for some minimum amount of calling whether you call or not. It's like the service charge levied by your bank for the "privilege" of carrying, but not using, your Visa card. While a flat monthly fee is always added to your actual calling charges, a minimum monthly usage requirement adds nothing to your bill if you satisfy your monthly minimum.

As a general rule, unless you have monthly long-distance bills of at least $20, you should be wary of even a $5 monthly minimum.

Is There a Volume Discount?

If you are a heavy long-distance caller, you may want a carrier that offers volume discounts. A number of the major carriers, including ITT, MCI, GTE Sprint, Western Union, and Allnet, have such discounts. The more you call, the larger the discount, gener-ally. Some carriers allow you a discount on the entire bill if your calling surpasses a certain level. Others only apply the discount to calls that exceed a specified amount.

Will the Calls You Make Travel "On-Net" or "Off-Net," and Will That Make a Difference in the Price?

Telephone networks aren't built in a day. For companies like MCI and GTE Sprint, the process of constructing transmission systems to compete with AT&T is both painstaking and expensive. Executives we know at MCI view their billion-dollar-a-year campaign to build a long-distance network that will be more state-of-the-art than AT&T's as something of a crusade. Nevertheless, none of the alternative carriers are capable yet of sending all their calls over their own network. To compensate for this limitation, they lease transmission lines from competitors with facilities in areas where their own networks do not yet reach. Calls that they can complete on their own facilities are called "on-network." Calls that must use leased lines are called "off-network."

As a consumer, it may be important whether your carrier completes your call "on" or "off-net," for it's invariably true that off-net calls cost your carrier more to complete than on-net calls. Most of the major carriers today have "single-tier" pricing, in which the rates are the same for on- and off-net calls, but a number of the "resale carriers" pass through the higher costs of off-net calling through "multiple-tier" pricing. Before you sign up with a carrier that charges different rates for on- and off-net calling, ask whether the places you call most frequently are on or off the network.

What Does It Cost to Dial the Carrier's Local Access Number and Begin the Long-distance Calling Process?

To make a long-distance call, you must begin by dialing a local access number to be connected with a computer switch that will direct your call to its destination over facilities either owned or leased by your carrier. For AT&T there's never been a charge for that call to the local switch. The way SBS works, it also has no local charge. Once equal access reaches you, you will never have to pay for the call to the local switch. But meanwhile, if you're using any carrier other than AT&T or SBS, you'll be billed for your call to the local switch. That's not a problem if you have flat-rate local service, but if you're a measured-service subscriber, the call will cost you message units. Depending on where you're calling from, that could add ten cents or more to the price of your long-distance call. Should the local switch be at the opposite end of the community from where you are located, the local calling costs could be considerably larger.

How Are Calls Timed?

Because of the kind of connections that most long-distance carriers receive from the local telephone company before equal access, it is impossible for most carriers to know exactly how long you are on the line. (Only AT&T and SBS are exceptions to this.) To get around this problem, carriers use a number of electronic techniques to measure your talking time. Rather than try to bill to the exact second, they bill in time units that afford some leeway in their estimates. AT&T, GTE Sprint, ITT, MCI, and Western Union all round to the next-highest full minute, for instance, while SBS and Allnet both round up to the next six-second interval after the first calling minute. The billing procedures a carrier uses can mean as much to you as a company's rates per minute. The fact that Western Union's rate on a particular route may be slightly lower than Allnet's may be irrelevant if Western Union rounds up to the next full minute while Allnet charges you for no more than an extra six seconds.

Can You Make Intrastate Long-distance Calls on the Carrier?

For arcane technological reasons the answer usually is yes, but neither the carriers nor your state regulatory authorities may tell you this. Here's why:

Before the breakup of AT&T, local telephone service was provided by the local operating companies while interstate long-distance service was the province of AT&T and the alternative long-distance carriers. As the only carrier authorized to provide intrastate long-distance service, AT&T had to adhere to rate levels set by state regulatory commissions. But because of legal ambiguities and technological complications, most of the alternative carriers provided intrastate long-distance service at discount rates as well.

When AT&T was broken up, a major monkey wrench was thrown into this scheme. To define the mission of the local telephone companies, the architects of divestiture divided the country into 162 calling zones, which they thought represented natural patterns of communication and commerce. In the Newspeak of the legal and technical world, these zones were called "Local Access and Transport Areas," or LATAs. The local telephone companies received the franchise for providing service within these LATAs on an *exclusive* basis. While much of this intra-LATA service is what we normally would think of as local in nature, some LATAs cover an entire state. Since a third of all long-distance traffic is intrastate, this meant that a large portion of the business that the long-distance carriers had previously had to themselves now belonged to the local operating companies.

In states with more than one LATA, AT&T is the only carrier that currently enjoys the authority to provide intrastate long-distance service between LATAs, but AT&T's major competitors are all petitioning the regulatory authorities in most states for permission to offer such service. In some cases, these carriers are even asking to provide intra-LATA service as well. There should be decisions on these petitions from every state by the end of 1985. Most state regulatory bodies are expected to permit carrier competition for intrastate service between LATA's, but to continue to insist on monopoly status for their local telephone companies within LATA's.

Meanwhile, the alternative carriers are providing intrastate inter-LATA service as they always have. The carriers don't publicize it, but unlike AT&T they won't have the technical wherewithal to determine where a call is originated until equal access arrives. As a result, they can't really tell whether you are using them to call interstate or intrastate; which means that you'll be able to take advantage of their discount rates on intrastate as well as interstate long-distance calls. Once equal access is introduced to your community, it will be easier to monitor this "shadow-calling" and your hidden benefit may end. Until then enjoy the ride!

Can You Use the Service to Call from Out of Town?

When you're on the road but want to be in touch, being able to call your home or office conveniently may be important to you. If you're calling on AT&T, that convenience bears a hefty price, however. While AT&T gives you the option of using a credit card, calling collect, or billing a call to a third number when you're away from home, there is a service charge of over a dollar to use an AT&T credit card and a charge of over $1.50 to bill a call to a third party.

A number of alternative carriers have travel features that allow you to call from places other than your own phone for less than what it would cost to use AT&T. A travel feature can be worthwhile even if you don't travel much. Suppose, for example, that you're at a neighbor's for dinner and must make a long-distance call. A travel feature enables you to call from your host's phone and yet have the conversation billed to your own account.

In areas where there is still unequal access, making a long-distance call from down the street involves exactly the same procedure as calling from home, on one of the alternative carriers. Just dial the 21- or 22-digit code that you would normally use to reach an alternative carrier's switch from your own phone. The carrier will treat the call as if you have made it from your home phone.

After equal access, you will still begin any calls made from another phone in your home city by dialing in a carrier access code, followed by your account number and the party you are calling. You will recall, however, that with equal access, the amount of dialing required to make a long-distance call from your own phone will be reduced substantially.

Carriers with travel features handle out-of-town calling in several different ways. Some give you local phone numbers for their switches in various cities and assign you a special identification number to use when calling from the road. Others provide an "800" number that connects you with their central switch, no matter where you are. Don't assume that all carriers will have travel features, or that all travel features are created equal. Some companies don't allow any calling from out of town; others only permit it in certain cities.

The companies also bill for their travel features in different ways. While some of the alternative carriers follow AT&T's example and bill credit card callers on a per-call basis, others impose an extra monthly fee or have higher charges per minute for travel feature calls.

As a footnote to this discussion, we should mention that AT&T issues a "Call Me" credit card that will only call back to your number if you wish. If you're a parent with children who have become strangers since they went off to college, or you have employees from whom you would like to hear regularly, you might consider giving them one of these cards on the next full moon.

Is the Transmission Quality Good Enough to Meet Your Needs?

Before the advent of equal access, using an alternative long-distance carrier was "low-rent" in two ways. By subscribing to one of AT&T's competitors, you could often save as much as 50 percent on your long-distance calls. But the trade-off for such savings was transmission quality that often made your calls sound as if they were coming from 20,000 leagues under the sea—or the next galaxy. One executive we know told his lawyers to stop calling him on an alternative carrier because he could never hear what they were saying. In our office, the long-distance carrier that our company subscribed to provided such poor connections that many of us abandoned the service and fell back on AT&T whenever we had an important call to make.

As we reported earlier, once equal access arrives in your community, many, if not all, of the alternative carriers should be able to hold their own with AT&T on transmission quality. One or two may even do better than AT&T. But it will be at least another year before many exchanges receive equal access, and even then, there will be carriers that lack the equipment or personnel to provide quality service, or that rely on a transmission technology that, in certain situations, can cause complications. When a company is transmitting by satellite, for instance, it takes a quarter-second to beam a conversation from the ground to a satellite approximately 22,000 miles above the equator, and another quarter-second to bounce the signal to its earthly destination. As a result, any time there are two voices trying to talk across the line at once, both voices get clipped slightly in the satellite transmission so that neither can be heard for an instant. If you don't interrupt your friends, that shouldn't be a problem.

For consumers who are worried about the quality of alternative carriers, there is an easy way to protect yourself. Just don't be in a hurry to select a primary carrier when equal access arrives in your neighborhood. You have six months from the time your exchange actually switches to equal access to make your choice without a charge, and you can test the quality of several alternative carriers during that period by using the five-digit access code that each of the carriers has been assigned.

Since it costs only $5 to change carriers, if you don't like the first company you select, we don't think your risk is very great, even if you skip the test-calling. We'd feel perfectly comfortable subscribing to one of the larger alternative carriers offering dial-up service on a national basis, without comparative testing. As we noted earlier, there will probably be several companies eager to pay the $5 charge for you to switch, should you wish to do so.

"Reach Out America" and "Opportunity Calling"

In the immediate aftermath of divestiture, the big rap against AT&T on Wall Street was that after a century of operating as a monopoly, it wouldn't know how to market aggressively. No sooner had the bell been rung down on the old Bell System than AT&T began to challenge that assumption with two special marketing programs for its long-distance customers: "Reach Out America" and "Opportunity Calling." Because of the wide promotion that these programs are receiving from AT&T, we felt we had to address them here. In doing so, we do not mean to endorse AT&T's products over the wealth of other marketing stratagems from AT&T's competitors.

The concepts for both Reach Out America and Opportunity Calling are beguilingly simple. Reach Out America allows you to call anywhere in the United States during night/weekend hours for $10 monthly. Those hours are from 11 P.M. to 8 A.M. daily, and include all day Saturday, and Sunday until 5 P.M. On a per-minute basis, Reach Out America works out to sixteen cents per minute. After the first sixty minutes, additional minutes cost fourteen-and-a-half cents per minute. For another $1.50 per month, you can also receive a fifteen-percent discount off AT&T's normal evening rates, which run from 5 P.M. to 11 P.M., Sunday through Friday.

At sixteen cents per minute, Reach Out America's rate is very competitive with what you'll find on many routes with alternative carriers. But keep in mind that the $10-per-month charge is a flat monthly charge, which means that you'll be billed $10 whether you call that much or not. Seventy-three percent of residential customers have long-distance bills of less than $10 per month. Even if you spend at least $10 per month, there may be cheaper ways for you to call on other carriers, or even on AT&T. In studying the initial results of Reach Out America, AT&T discovered that 30 percent of its participants would have been better off using AT&T's standard direct-distance dialing service to do their calling. So look before you leap.

With Opportunity Calling, your long-distance calls earn you points that can be applied to the purchase of consumer items and services listed in a special catalogue distributed by AT&T every three months. Under the plan, AT&T doesn't sell you the catalogue merchandise itself. Rather, it mails you credit vouchers which you can apply to the purchase price at any retail establishment carrying the product in question. One recent catalogue offered residential telephone customers discounts on everything from stereo equipment to Caribbean cruises and Ryder truck rentals.

If your principal concern is lower phone bills, Opportunity Calling does nothing at all to solve that problem. As one consumer advocate suggested to us, Opportunity Calling is basically "a kickback" for doing your calling on AT&T. Some of you may well prefer the booty being offered, as opposed to a lower phone bill. We're stodgy enough to want to keep our mashed potatoes and our ice cream separate on our plates.

Seeking Outside Help

If you still have questions or need help after reading *Teleshock*, there are several consumer groups that stand ready to lend assistance. The Telecommunications Research and Action Center (TRAC), P.O. Box 12038, Washington, D.C. 20005, is a national membership organization whose ambition is to become the American Automobile Association of telephone users. It has teamed up with the Consumer Federation of America to operate a Tele-Consumer Hotline to answer consumer questions about the telephone. If you call the hotline and ask for information on long-distance companies in your area, they'll tell you exactly what your choices are and the features they offer. They will not do rate comparisons for you, however, since that information changes so rapidly. In the mid-Atlantic states the hotline number is 800-332-1124. The service isn't available everywhere yet, so check to see if it, or perhaps an affiliate, is operating in your area.

The Center for the Study of Services, whose work we've mentioned in an earlier chapter, has developed a computer program to analyze long-distance bills. It includes about forty companies operating all over the country, and the organizers promise it will cover five out of every six long-distance companies operating in each market. For a fee, Checkbook will analyze your phone bill and send you a computer printout of how much your calls would cost on the long-distance companies operating in your area.

The service isn't cheap, but it's a way to analyze your phone expenses systematically. To use the service, send the long-distance portion of a fairly typical phone bill or bills (up to three months'), along with a check based on the size of your highest bill (see Table 10), payable to "Checkbook," and addressed as follows: CHECK-BOOK's Computerized Long-distance Comparison, 806 Fifteenth Street, N.W., Suite 925, Washington, D.C. 20005.

TABLE 10
Checkbook Phone Analysis Fee Schedule

If the highest bill you send is	Checkbook's fee is
$10 or less	$10
$10.01 to $20	$15
$20.01 to $30	$20
$30.01 to $40	$25
$40.01 to $70	$30
$70.01 to $100	$40
$100.01 to $300	$75
Over $300	Ask about Checkbook's consulting service.

One last bit of advice: Choosing a long-distance company shouldn't be as agonizing as buying a car, a washing machine, or any other major appliance. You've got lots of time to think things out, try out the system, and then make your choice. With equal access being phased in gradually across the country, rates are going to be in a state of flux for some time.

In the end, the telephone long-distance business may turn out to be much like the airline industry, where rates are almost always the same for carriers on the same routes. Like that industry, many of the long-distance companies competing today may not survive the squeeze between their prices and their costs. Some people are already planning on it. One large telephone company is working on a long-range plan based on the premise that by the early 1990s there will be only two providers of long-distance service in this country—AT&T and IBM.

TABLE 11
Long-distance Carrier Features

Company	Startup Fee	Minimum Bill	Call Timed	Travel Feature	Credit Cards*	Sign-up, Information
Allnet	none	none	by 6 seconds after 1st min.	yes	AE, V, MC	800-982-8888
AT&T	none	none	by 1 min.	yes	AE (on Card Caller phones)	800-222-0300 home 800-222-0400 business
Sprint	none	$5/month	by 1 min.	yes	no	800-521-4949
ITT	none	none	by 1 min.	yes	no	800-526-3000
MCI	none	none	by 1 min.	yes	AE, V, MC	800-624-2010
SBS	none	$15/month	by 6 seconds after 1st min.	yes	no	800-235-2001
Western Union	none	$10/month	by 1 min.	yes	V, MC	800-526-7878 non-business hours

*AE = American Express
V = Visa
MC = MasterCard

4

Coping with Bills, Cranks, and Emergencies

CHAPTER 11 How to Read Your Phone Bill—and Complain

Nowhere does the confusion of divestiture hit home more forcefully than when you try to decipher your monthly phone bill. Where once there was a simple monthly bill from "the phone company" that included all your local and long-distance service charges and equipment rental fees, the bill, or bills, that you receive now are beginning to look like short novels—mystery novels, some would say.

Now that telephone service has been broken into three parts—local service, long-distance, and equipment—the number of pipers that must be paid at the end of the month has increased threefold. For local telephone service there is your local operating company to be reckoned with. If you are still renting your telephone equipment, AT&T Information Systems has a claim on you. Your long-distance tab will be with either AT&T's long-distance division, AT&T Communications, or one of the alternative long-distance carriers such as MCI, GTE Sprint, or SBS.

In some areas of the country, AT&T is still billing through its former operating company subsidiaries. In those cases, your local telephone company will bill you not only for local service, but also for any equipment rentals or long-distance service provided to you by AT&T. In many places, however, ATT Information Systems is now doing its own billing for equipment charges, and on the long-distance side, ATT Communications is considering similar plans. Meanwhile, most of the alternative long-distance carriers bill their customers separately each month. While some may decide that it is more cost-effective to have the local telephone company bill for them, most people are likely to have to deal with three different bills for monthly telephone service before long, if they are not already.

If you think you're confused by the new billing system, don't feel badly. As telephone industry regulator William Shane of the Pennsylvania Public Utilities Commission testified recently, "If this commissioner with a Harvard degree in economics and a law degree and almost eight years' working experience at the PUC, and hopefully, with average intelligence, has trouble understanding his home phone bill, then probably there are other Pennsylvanians with similar difficulties."

To help you decipher the billing mystery, we've included, on the following pages, a sample telephone bill with captions explaining what each category means.

How to Deal with Billing and Other Problems

Phone companies don't like to admit it, but the bills they send out each month often contain problems. No one really knows just how frequent the problems are, since phone bills are probably among the most detailed, and therefore least carefully examined, bills we receive as consumers. The fact that there are now more companies providing telephone service than ever before, and that many of these companies issue their own bills, means that there are now more bills on which errors can be made than ever before.

_____ **TABLE 12** _____
Telephone Bills Explained

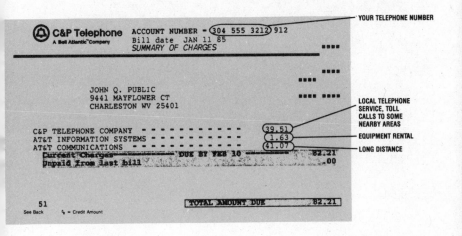

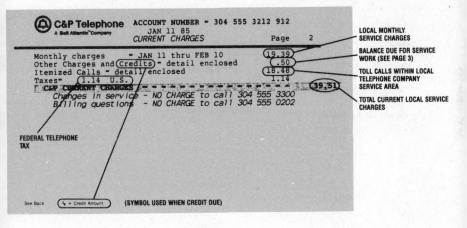

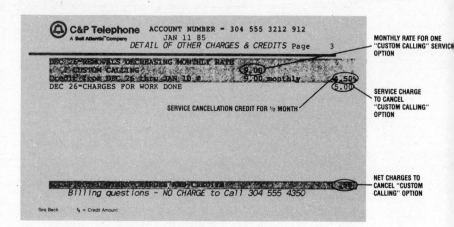

MONTHLY RATE FOR ONE "CUSTOM CALLING" SERVICE OPTION

SERVICE CHARGE TO CANCEL "CUSTOM CALLING" OPTION

SERVICE CANCELLATION CREDIT FOR ½ MONTH

NET CHARGES TO CANCEL "CUSTOM CALLING" OPTION

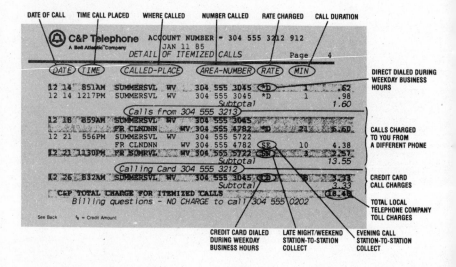

DATE OF CALL   TIME CALL PLACED   WHERE CALLED   NUMBER CALLED   RATE CHARGED   CALL DURATION

DIRECT DIALED DURING WEEKDAY BUSINESS HOURS

CALLS CHARGED TO YOU FROM A DIFFERENT PHONE

CREDIT CARD CALL CHARGES

TOTAL LOCAL TELEPHONE COMPANY TOLL CHARGES

CREDIT CARD DIALED DURING WEEKDAY BUSINESS HOURS

LATE NIGHT/WEEKEND STATION-TO-STATION COLLECT

EVENING CALL STATION-TO-STATION COLLECT

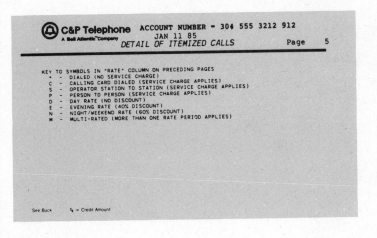

C&P Telephone
A Bell Atlantic Company

ACCOUNT NUMBER - 304 555 3212 912
JAN 11 85
DETAIL OF ITEMIZED CALLS   Page   5

KEY TO SYMBOLS IN "RATE" COLUMN ON PRECEDING PAGES
- • - DIALED (NO SERVICE CHARGE)
- C - CALLING CARD DIALED (SERVICE CHARGE APPLIES)
- S - OPERATOR STATION TO STATION (SERVICE CHARGE APPLIES)
- P - PERSON TO PERSON (SERVICE CHARGE APPLIES)
- D - DAY RATE (NO DISCOUNT)
- E - EVENING RATE (40% DISCOUNT)
- N - NIGHT/WEEKEND RATE (60% DISCOUNT)
- M - MULTI-RATED (MORE THAN ONE RATE PERIOD APPLIES)

See Back   ↳ = Credit Amount

FEDERAL TELEPHONE TAX   **STATE TELEPHONE TAX**

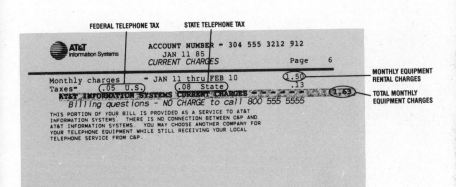

AT&T Information Systems

ACCOUNT NUMBER - 304 555 3212 912
JAN 11 85
CURRENT CHARGES   Page   6

Monthly charges - JAN 11 thru FEB 10   1.50 ——— **MONTHLY EQUIPMENT RENTAL CHARGES**
Taxes- .05 U.S.   .08 State   .13
AT&T INFORMATION SYSTEMS CURRENT CHARGES ─ ─ ─ ─ ─ ─ ─ ─   1.63 ——— **TOTAL MONTHLY EQUIPMENT CHARGES**
Billing questions - NO CHARGE to call 800 555 5555

THIS PORTION OF YOUR BILL IS PROVIDED AS A SERVICE TO AT&T
INFORMATION SYSTEMS. THERE IS NO CONNECTION BETWEEN C&P AND
AT&T INFORMATION SYSTEMS. YOU MAY CHOOSE ANOTHER COMPANY FOR
YOUR TELEPHONE EQUIPMENT WHILE STILL RECEIVING YOUR LOCAL
TELEPHONE SERVICE FROM C&P.

See Back   ↳ = Credit Amount

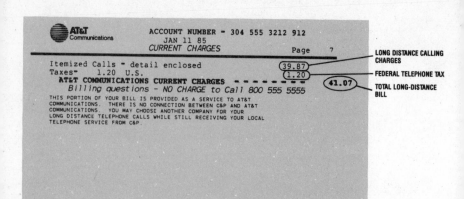

LONG DISTANCE CALLING CHARGES

FEDERAL TELEPHONE TAX

TOTAL LONG-DISTANCE BILL

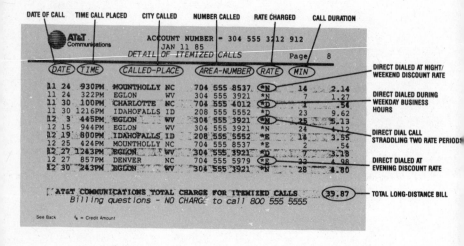

DATE OF CALL   TIME CALL PLACED   CITY CALLED   NUMBER CALLED   RATE CHARGED   CALL DURATION

DIRECT DIALED AT NIGHT/WEEKEND DISCOUNT RATE

DIRECT DIALED DURING WEEKDAY BUSINESS HOURS

DIRECT DIAL CALL STRADDLING TWO RATE PERIODS

DIRECT DIALED AT EVENING DISCOUNT RATE

TOTAL LONG-DISTANCE BILL

ACCOUNT NUMBER = 304 555 3212 912
JAN 11 85
DETAIL OF ITEMIZED CALLS   Page   9

KEY TO SYMBOLS IN "RATE" COLUMN ON PRECEDING PAGES
*   -   DIALED (NO SERVICE CHARGE)
C   -   CALLING CARD DIALED (SERVICE CHARGE APPLIES)
S   -   OPERATOR STATION TO STATION (SERVICE CHARGE APPLIES)
P   -   PERSON TO PERSON (SERVICE CHARGE APPLIES)
D   -   DAY RATE (NO DISCOUNT)
E   -   EVENING RATE (40% DISCOUNT)
N   -   NIGHT/WEEKEND RATE (60% DISCOUNT)
M   -   MULTI-RATED (MORE THAN ONE RATE PERIOD APPLIES)
A   -   PART OF CALL CONTAINED IN SPEC LONG DISTANCE CALLING SVC
R   -   OVERSEAS STANDARD RATE (NO DISCOUNT)
T   -   OVERSEAS DISCOUNT RATE (25% LESS THAN STANDARD)
Y   -   OVERSEAS ECONOMY RATE (40% LESS THAN STANDARD)
ABOVE SYMBOLS DO NOT APPLY TO CALLS TO OR FROM ALASKA OR HAWAII

See Back   ⌐ = Credit Amount

You are the most basic protection you have against such mistakes. Scrutinize your bill carefully when it comes in each month. If you don't read your bill before paying it, there is no way in the world you can shield yourself from being victimized by telephone billing problems.

In examining your local phone bill, pay close attention to the charges billed to you for changes in the kind of service you have been receiving from the telephone company. If you have recently added or eliminated a phone line, signed up for special calling features such as Call Waiting or Call Forwarding, or had a repair person to your house for wiring work, make sure you are being charged for what you received and nothing more. Billing errors crop up much more frequently when you've changed your service than when there's nothing different from the previous month.

If you still rent phones from AT&T Information Systems (AT&T IS), be certain that you are not being billed for more instruments than you actually possess. Check your equipment charges especially carefully if you have recently returned a telephone to AT&T IS and should be seeing your monthly equipment bill reduced to reflect this. All too often you will find AT&T IS billing you for *more,* rather than fewer, phones the following month.

On your long-distance bill, pay special attention to calls billed to your credit card or charged to your number by a third party at a distant location. Be sure that the calls were yours or you know who made them and you approve. If you are using an alternative long-distance carrier, thoroughly check the numbers called, because it is disturbingly easy for someone to guess your five- or six-digit access code while searching randomly for a carrier access code that will enable him or her to make long-distance calls for free.

Watch also for very short long-distance calls. Since it's difficult for the alternative carriers to tell if or when the party you are calling answers in unequal access areas, the alternative carriers usually begin billing you after thirty or forty seconds if you have not hung up the line. (See Chapter 10 for more on this.) But many of these companies won't charge you for uncompleted calls if you tell them that your call was never answered. To receive this waiver, you have to let the carrier know, however. If you just sit back and expect your carrier to cut your bill on its own, it won't happen.

When you have a problem with any part of your monthly bill,

look at the telephone number listed on the bill to call for billing problems, and use it. If the problem is with your local bill, call the number given for local billing questions. If it's an equipment issue, dial the number provided for AT&T IS.

Many of the alternative long-distance carriers allow you to correct mistaken charges yourself, simply by crossing out calls on your bill that you did not make and subtracting the amount of those calls from your check when you pay. To protest billing errors by AT&T's long-distance service, look for the 800-number provided on the bill for billing problems and call that number. It's very important to realize that it won't do any good to call your local telephone company about an equipment or long-distance billing problem, even if the local operating company performs the billing function for your long-distance carrier or equipment provider. You must call the company with which you have the question.

Whenever you have a problem with the telephone company, keep notes of the person to whom you talk, what is said, and when your call(s) are made, so that you will have a record if the telephone company is slow to take care of your objection. If you're unhappy with the attention you're getting, don't just ask to speak with a supervisor. Escalate quickly by demanding to speak to a vice-president or similarly high-ranking official. The higher up the corporate ladder you get initially, the faster your complaint is likely to be resolved. Always remember: THE SQUEAKY WHEEL GETS THE GREASE.

One veteran telephone company official we know suggests that if you have a problem involving your local Bell operating company, the best way to get action is to call a senior executive and tell the executive's secretary that you have important business to discuss with the boss, without specifying what that business might be. Tell the secretary that you will hold the line until the executive is free. Told that someone is on the phone with urgent business, few executives will dare keep you waiting long.

When you get the executive on the line, state your complaint forcefully. Indicate that you will protest to the state public utility commission (PUC) if necessary. Threatening to complain to the state PUC may not have much effect at lower levels, but senior executives take such warnings very seriously. Never invoke the name of the PUC unless you are willing to follow through on your threat, however. If the executive doesn't "cause" your problem to be taken care of with reasonable speed, write the executive a follow-up letter, clearly indicating that you are sending a copy of the letter to the PUC. Even in this day of instant electronic communication, a letter commands a lot of attention.

To be effective in dealing with the phone company, it's extremely helpful to know your rights. If your dispute is over rates or services, the answer to what you're entitled to is usually in the papers, or tariffs, that the phone company must file with the regulators. While these tariffs can sometimes be as obtuse as hieroglyphics, it's worth asking your state PUC which tariff applies in your case. If you want to look at a tariff yourself, you'll find them all on file at your local telephone company business office and in many cities at the local public library.

State PUCs generally have consumer representatives whose job is to mediate your dispute with the local telephone company. Call and ask for one to help you. You will find telephone numbers and addresses for all fifty state PUCs in the Appendix at the back of this book.

If your dispute is with a long-distance carrier, the complaint process is the same. Try established channels first, but if you don't get quick attention, go up the executive ladder.

12 Harassment and Emergencies

W hen you think about it, the telephone is a pretty miraculous little piece of work. Just a few bits of plastic and metal hanging on your wall or sitting on your desk or counter can put you in touch, within seconds, with just about anybody, anywhere in the world, even if the call literally has to go out of this world via satellite to be completed.

Unfortunately, the technology that gives you such freedom to "reach out and touch someone," also gives other people the ability to do the same to you. That's all right if those calling are friends or other people with whom you'd like to speak. But often the telephone can be used to harass, abuse, or even frighten people who otherwise want to be left alone. In those cases, you need some different telephone skills from the ones you normally use.

Consider this statistic: four out of every ten burglaries in homes occur where the door is unlocked. In other words, 40 percent of the households said, in effect, "Here, just come on in and rip me off." It was almost like an open invitation, even if an inadvertent one, to a burglar. That's an important principle to bear in mind when dealing with people who make obscene or threatening or otherwise harassing telephone calls to your telephone.

Contrary to what you might expect, telephone harassment is rarely initiated by "dirty old men." In fact, some studies have shown that many harassing calls are made by women. Bored teenagers and unattended youngsters looking for a little excitement are also frequent perpetrators.

If you get such a call, the police advise just one thing: hang up. That's it. No conversation, no cussing, no threatening. Just hang up. Police experts say that the people who make these calls have one motivation: to get your attention. You don't want to give it to them. You control your telephone; it is not controlled by someone at the other end of the line. If the person on the other end is quiet for too long or says something obscene or threatening, hang up immediately.

It sounds simple enough, just a matter of common sense. But one of our police sources, officer Tom Coffman of the Montgomery County, Maryland Crime Prevention Unit, says the hardest thing to teach people is to hang up the phone. "You don't want to initiate contact. That's what [the callers] are looking for," Coffman says. Some people try to deal with the situation by psychoanalyzing the caller or by carrying on an extended conversation. One woman reported to police that she had been getting obscene calls from the same caller for three years. She had talked with the man for two hours at a time, trying to make him stop. In the course of those conversations she had given him her name, address, and other information. Not smart. Talking to the caller is like leaving the door open for the burglar—it gives him the opening he wants. Adults in the house shouldn't give out any information. Children should be instructed not to give out your name or address, and anyone staying in the house, whether babysitters for an evening or relatives or friends for longer periods of time, should follow the same precautions.

If some people are reluctant to hang up the phone, there is even more reluctance to take the phone off the hook or otherwise tie it up in order to discourage callers. Don't feel this way. Our police sources advise that if someone wants to get an emergency call through to you, they will, either by contacting a neighbor, or by calling back later, or, if all else fails, by asking the police to drop by your house with a message.

Should the problem calls continue, make a log of them and report them to the police and the telephone company, who will work together on a plan to trace the calls. You should also consider changing the way you list your telephone number. Because women are often the targets of crank callers, many single women try to protect themselves by only listing their names by their first initials. While that keeps a woman's first name from being disclosed, if all the other listings have names, and only one has just an initial, it's a good bet that the listing with the initial is a woman.

From a security standpoint, the police suggest that it would be far better, if you are a single woman, not to list your name at all. Your family and friends have your number. You can give it to anyone you want to have it. Someone you know will find a way to get in touch with you, if necessary, through a mutual friend or business associate. Why make yourself a target?

Not listing addresses is also a good precaution against burglaries. It's possible that a burglar can find a likely candidate for a break-in by phoning homes from a cross-reference directory to determine which homes on a particular street are occupied. But in reality, police say most break-ins are caused by burglars cruising down streets looking for empty houses; they seldom call in advance.

How you deal with junk telephone calls, surveys, sales pitches, and the like depends on your good nature and the value you put on your time. If you like talking to strangers, the caller on the other end of the line is being paid to indulge you. If you don't want to be bothered, say "Thank you," and firmly hang up. Once you respond to a telephone solicitation, your name goes on a list as someone who will deal with such calls. Like mailing lists that blitz you with unwanted mail, you will soon start getting lots of unwanted telephone inquiries.

If you think you might be interested, but are concerned about the caller's bona fides, ask the caller's name and phone number and request that you be mailed additional information that you can peruse at your leisure. A legitimate caller will be glad to oblige. In our households, the one inviolable rule is: the salesperson who calls at dinnertime talks only to the dog.

So far, we've focused on how to react to phone calls that

invade your privacy. But at other times there is no more valuable device in all the world than the telephone. In emergency situations it can literally save your life. Faced with such a crisis, you can get help quickly in two ways:

• Dial 911. In most places, dialing 911 will get you the police, fire department, and rescue service. Be sure to give your name, address, phone number and the type of assistance you need as calmly as you can, so that the police, ambulance, or fire department will know what to do when they get to your house. Be sure to give the information in as calm a tone as possible. If you have a telephone that can store numbers electronically, be sure to designate one for police and fire. (For automatic fire, burglar, and other alarms, see Chapter 18.)

• Dial *0*. In an emergency situation, even remembering to dial 911 may be difficult. It's comforting to know that you can still dial the familiar *0* for operator—even with divestiture. The operators work for AT&T, but your local phone company pays AT&T to provide local operator service. Just tell the operator it's an emergency. The operator will do the rest.

5

Beyond P.O.T.S. (Plain Old Telephone Service)

CHAPTER 13 Answering Machines

There is no logical reason why the decision to purchase a relatively simple electronic device should be turned into a metaphysical debate over the nature of humanity—except when the device in question is a telephone answering machine. Not your ordinary convenience product, answering machines have the capacity to split society into two emotional groups.

For the sake of arguments, we'll call the first group "Luddites" in tribute to the nineteenth-century English textile workers who smashed factory machinery they blamed for high unemployment. Their view of the world, which they defend as "humanist," goes like this: "When I call a person, I want to talk to a person, not a damned machine. There's nothing worse than to call somebody, hear 'Hi,' start to talk, and then feel like an idiot because you're talking to a tape. And I hate that damned beep."

A second group called, again for the sake of argument, the "Progressives," also sees its view of the world as "humanist." The Progressive argument goes like this: "My friends and associates mean a lot to me. I don't think it's asking too much for them to listen to a few seconds of tape and then leave a message. Having an answering machine means I don't have to be tied down waiting for a phone call. That's important, particularly when I'm out looking for work."

You're free to choose a side in this great existential debate, but you should know that the Progressives seem to be winning. Sales of answering machines have grown from 850,000 in 1982 to 2.2 million in 1983, to 2.7 million in 1984, with projected sales of 3.5 million for 1985, according to the Electronic Industries Association (EIA).

A good reason for that trend is shown by the EIA figures for price. The average price for an answering machine was $129 in 1982. It will be only about $83 in 1985, EIA estimates. In 1984, the telephone-answering-device business will be worth about $440 million, according to one leading answering-machine maker. Even with those impressive figures, there's still a lot of room for growth because most of those sales were to business users. There are answering machines in only about 7 percent of the homes in the country, and the industry expects that figure to expand as the price comes down and the machines become easier to use. Changes in American ways of living are also likely to boost demand for answering machines, as more and more women go to work and as the number of singles living alone increases.

By this point, you should have some feeling as to where your sympathies lie. If you are still a dedicated Luddite, then forget the rest of this chapter, and find something else to read. Step into the shower and hope somebody doesn't call. But if you are a wavering Luddite, a dedicated Progressive, or just curious, let us tell you what types of machines are out there, and what you can get for your money. The industry has grown so fast in the last few years that there are now about 500 listings of answering machines and related items on file with the Federal Communications Commission's equipment registration program.

A bottom-of-the-line answering machine today costs about $50. All such a machine will do is answer calls. It will not put out a message from you. Spend $100, and your options increase dramatically. For $100, you can get a machine that has a voice-activated tape and call monitor, allows you to set the ring on which the answering machine will answer, and has a remote unit to let you call from another phone to check your recorded messages. For about $200, you can get an answering machine that allows you to hear your messages by calling home from another telephone, and for a little more money, you can get a fancy machine with a telephone attached.

Answering Machine Features

Before you rush out to your local electronics store, department store, or bargain basement to get the phone machine of your choice and budget, take a look at some of the options you can get:

• Audio scan. Allows the machine to search through a message tape and play messages only, skipping over calls that didn't leave a message.

• Beeper remote control. A beeper remote unit is a little electronic device about the size of a cigarette pack that allows you to get messages from your answering machine when you are not at home. To use it, call your home phone, and put the beeper remote unit up to the telephone's mouthpiece. Push a button, and it emits a tone that signals your home answering machine to play back any messages on your tape at home.

• Beeperless remote control. The next step up in technology is the beeperless remote. The principle is the same as the beeper remote—you don't have to be home to hear your messages. But instead of carrying around a little signaling device, you need only to call your number from a tone phone and punch in a special code that tells your machine to play back the messages.

• Built-in telephone. Obvious, but keep in mind that some phones, even those that come with answering machines, have more features than other phones. Some answering machines come with ordinary phones, others with buttons that allow you to redial the last number with only one button or give you the capacity to program the telephone to dial numbers by pushing only one button.

• Dual-cassette. A basic answering machine is nothing more than two tape recorders put together in one box. One tape cassette contains your outgoing message: "Hello, I'm not home . . ." The other cassette records messages from your callers.

• Ring-select. If you are asleep and don't want to be bothered with a ringing telephone, but do want to catch calls, your machine can answer the telephone on the first or second ring. This is also a courtesy to your callers. If you're home and want to give yourself a chance to get to the phone, you can set it to pick up after five or six rings.

• Toll-saver. Let's say you travel a lot and want to check on your messages at home. It's an expensive and wasteful process to call your answering machine with a long-distance call, only to find you don't have any messages. Toll-saver, found on expensive machines, allows you to call your home phone and have the answering machine screen the tape before completing the call and before it costs you any money. One model answers the phone after the second ring if there are messages for you; if there are no messages, it doesn't answer till the fourth ring.

• Variable outgoing message. One of the newest high-tech features, variable outgoing message lets you program your answering machine to put out one message at one time of day, another message later on.

• Voice activation for incoming calls. Some Luddite friend may call you up, hear the tape start, and hang up. With a voice-activated tape, your answering machine won't start to record until a caller speaks. With other devices, the tape starts as soon as the machine cuts in, leaving a tape full of blurps and buzzes.

• Voice synthesis. Voice synthesis substitutes your personalized outgoing message recorded on tape with an electronic one built into the machine. Instead of two tapes, the machine has a microchip that allows the phone to answer in its own "friendly, electronic voice" (as the manufacturer describes it), and then takes a message. Toshiba is using voice synthesis in its TCB 50 model to tell a machine owner how many calls there are, and on what day and time they arrived.

Do you need all of those fancy features? Probably not. For your everyday homebody, there's no need for beeperless remote or variable messages. Just a simple dual-cassette box with voice activation is all most people need. After that, it's up to your whim and wallet. But if you travel or use your home as an office, then you might want to consider some of the more exotic features.

Some manufacturers are simplifying how answering machines work while at the same time adding more features and bringing down prices. Instead of a choice between the basic two-tape machine, or a single-cassette machine that does half the job, one company is coming out with a single microcassette model that will record both your outgoing message and incoming calls, without erasing either. It will be small enough to put on the wall, so you won't have to take up desk space or table space or hide the thing in a drawer.

One of the hottest telephone trends these days is cellular phones (Chapter 15). Answering machine makers are looking eagerly to the day when car phones are accompanied by answering machines. Marketers believe that people who buy cellular phones consider their calls important, so they may be willing to spend a little more money to make sure they don't miss any calls. The Luddites will truly hate this development. If the person they call doesn't answer, his car will.

Buying Tips

By now, you should have some definite ideas about answering machines. If you decide to buy one, here are some hints:

• Buy only what you need. All that good gadgetry is fun, but if you don't need it, why bother? Remote control is fine if you're away a lot, but if you come home at night, you can save money by selecting a regular machine. If you don't receive, say, thirty calls a day, you don't need a machine with a large storage capacity.

• Don't buy a machine that looks too complex. These machines should be easy to use and to install, simply by plugging a modular jack from your phone into the machine, and the machine's plug into the phone jack in the wall.

• Check warranties carefully, not only from the manufacturer but also from the store that sells you the machine. A store warranty that allows you to return a defective machine and trade it in for a new one is much more helpful than a warranty that will get your machine fixed only if you send it away.

• Phrase your outgoing message carefully. Rather than say, "I'm not home now," and give a potential burglar a good head-start, say something like, "I can't come to the phone right now," which can mean anything—that you are in the shower or that you are 5,000 miles away.

• The most important point to remember when using a telephone answering machine is to *turn it on*. There's nothing more frustrat-

ing than to come home expecting an important call and find that the
machine has been sitting on your desk, dark, with no little call-
counter lights or anything. It may sound obvious, but how often do
you forget to turn off the lights when you leave?

• Fun. It's possible to amuse your callers, even Luddites, if you
dream up clever answering messages. There is one basic bit of
advice we have, however. Don't use the old, "Hi, this is Bill's
answering machine" opening. It makes even the most dedicated
Progressive cringe. Other than that, the field's open. Singing
messages can be effective. Since answering machine cassettes are
the same ones you play in your stereo, if you have a cassette deck,
you can use that machine's capabilities to add background music,
sound effects, and better-quality voice.

If you want some assistance, a New Jersey company, Phonies,
has signed up comedian Rich Little and comedienne Julie Dees to
give you a hand, or voice, as it were. Their "Phonies" tapes sell for
about $10 and have twelve messages on a tape, allowing your
telephone to be answered by impressions of Rod Serling, Richard
Nixon, Humphrey Bogart, Dolly Parton, Diana Ross or Greta
Garbo. For more information, contact Phonies, P.O. Box 2110,
Cherry Hill, NJ 08003. Their telephone number is 609-424-6787.
The day we called, a slightly suggestive Marilyn Monroe-sounding
tape ("Do you want to be beeped by me?") was playing on their
machine. It was almost enough to overcome a Luddite's opposi-
tion.

CHAPTER 14 Cordless Telephones

It is Saturday afternoon, and you want to work in your backyard rose garden. You are also waiting for an important telephone call. If the call comes through while you are pruning roses, you'll miss it. You could carry a standard telephone out to the garden on a very long extension cord so you can prune while you wait for the call. Or you could do what more than six million Americans did in 1984: buy a cordless telephone.

A cordless telephone is just that: an extension phone that uses radio instead of wires to connect the handset to the phone line. With a cordless telephone you can make and receive calls up to several hundred feet from the phone's base station in your house. How far it will reach depends on the quality of the phone and on local conditions. Almost any cordless phone will work from anywhere in your house. With a good-quality phone you ought to be able to talk from nearly anywhere in your yard. If your yard is so big that the signal from a cordless phone can't reach the farthest corners, don't worry; with a yard that size you can probably afford a $4000 portable cellular telephone. (For more information on the new cellular telephones, see Chapter 15.)

Cordless telephones come in two parts, a base station that is plugged into the telephone and electric power lines, and a battery-powered handset. When not in use, the handset is "hung up" on the base station, so it can be recharged—and so you know where it is. The base station is not only a telephone, it is a little radio station. The handset is also a radio, as you can tell from its stub antenna.

The base station transmits to the handset on one radio frequency, and the handset replies on another frequency. The base station of many cordless phones built before October 1, 1984, transmitted at a frequency of 1.7 megahertz. That's just above the top of the AM radio dial. If you have an older cordless phone, your neighbors who own AM sets may be able to hear your conversations. The base stations of all cordless telephones built after October 1, 1984, and some made before, transmit at a frequency of 46 megahertz, so that will eliminate the AM radio eavesdropping, as well as some sources of interference, such as power lines. That still doesn't guarantee privacy, however, for anyone with a short-wave radio or scanner able to listen at 46 or 49 megahertz (the frequency used by the handset) may be able to hear what you are saying.

Like all electronic devices, cordless phones get cheaper all the time. While it is possible to spend more than $250 for a cordless phone with every possible accessory, careful shopping can usually produce a cordless phone with most desired features for under $125.

Cordless Problems

As you stand in your rose garden talking on your cordless telephone, you'll be amazed at its convenience. But you should realize that it's a radio trying to function as a telephone. Radios can pick up interference from other sources. Your cordless phone may work well 95 percent of the time. But during that other 5 percent, you may get so much interference from television sets, computers, vacuum cleaners, power lines, and even other cordless telephones, that you have to resort to the old-fashioned wired telephone. For that reason, cordless phones should not be counted on as your primary instrument, but only as extension phones.

There are only ten frequencies available for all the cordless phones in the nation, which means that if your neighbor's cordless is set to the same channel as yours, the two phones may interfere with one another. The best way to eliminate interference is to change to another of the ten channels available. If your phone is fixed at one channel, you have little choice but to take it back to the dealer and swap it. Some phones allow you to "scan" through several channels, even while you are talking, to select the one that is the clearest. This is definitely a worthwhile feature. If you can't talk on your cordless, what good is it?

Although all cordless telephones manufactured after October 1, 1984, operate on 46 and 49 megahertz, older phones can still be sold and used. Unless you get an incredibly good deal on a phone that uses the 1.7 megahertz frequency, we'd advise you to pass it up.

There is an even more serious potential problem with cordless phones, and that is security. If your cordless telephone is an early model or has no protection, someone can come through your neighborhood with a cordless handset looking for dial tones from a base station. If he's able to get a dial tone from your base station, he can place calls to Tokyo or Paris on your line—and you'll never know it till you get your bill.

Fortunately, manufacturers have devised two ways that are very effective in eliminating theft of cordless phone service. Under the first scheme, the phone transmits an inaudible tone. If the base station doesn't recognize the tone, the call can't be completed. Under the second scheme, the base station and the handset are set to the same electronic code. The base station won't recognize any handset that doesn't broadcast this code, even if it is on the same frequency. You can usually set the code yourself. Some phones have a set of eight tiny switches, giving you 256 possible code combinations, while some manufacturers advertise 1000 or more codes. You don't need more than 256 combinations in your Rubik's Cube to do the job.

A third potential problem with cordless telephones is hearing damage. Many cordless phones, like many regular electronic phones, use the little speaker in the earphone as the ringer. That's not a problem with regular electronic phones. Once you pick up the handset, the phone is off the hook, and it can't ring again. But you pick up your cordless phone every time you move, so it has to be taken off the hook manually. When you are carrying your cordless phone around with you and it rings, you have to move a little switch in order to answer it. While you are waiting for a call, the switch is set to "standby." When the phone rings, you move the switch to "talk" and start your conversation. If you forget to move the switch, or don't know you are supposed to (as a small child might not), and you put the phone up to your ear—wham!—the phone rings directly in your ear. Since the ringer has to be loud enough to alert you from some distance away, you can imagine what a blast you get with the receiver up to your ear.

The Food and Drug Administration has received numerous complaints from people who claim their hearing has been damaged by cordless phones, and at least one court has awarded money to someone claiming that his hearing had been harmed by a cordless phone. It's possible that hearing can be harmed by noises that reach the 120-decibel level—an amplified rock band—and likely at 140 decibels. One medical study found that some cordless phones ring at a level of 137 to 141 decibels. To protect your hearing, avoid models in which the earphone doubles as the ringer, or look for models in which the manufacturer has moved the ringer speaker to the back side of the receiver where it's very unlikely to ring in someone's ear.

Despite these difficulties, cordless phones can be a real convenience. Careful shopping can eliminate or mitigate the most serious difficulties. Try out the phone in the store before you buy to make sure the voice quality is satisfactory (it's unlikely to be as good as a standard phone, but it should be close). Call a friend and ask him how you sound. When you look for a cordless phone, shop only at dealers that will allow you to exchange the phone, if necessary. It may turn out that certain cordless phones simply won't work where you live because there is too much interference.

Cordless Features

Cordless phones aren't second-class citizens when it comes to having bells and whistles. They offer many of the features available on other modern electronic telephones. Here are a few of the most popular options from which you can choose.

• Intercom. If you are working in your rose garden and someone in the house wishes to talk to you, all he or she needs to do is push a button on the base station to beep your phone. You move a switch to intercom to talk to the person inside. It can work the other way around, too. Push a button on the handset to beep the base station, then select intercom to holler, "Please come help me, I'm completely tangled up in the rose bushes!" Some phones offer paging only. One beep might mean come in for dinner, two beeps could mean, "I love you."

• Speakerphone. This annoyance from the business world is coming into the home and is available on some cordless models. It allows a conversation between a roomful of people—say, in your kitchen—and someone at the other end.

• Pulse/tone switch. This allows the phone to be used with either pulse- (which is the same as rotary) or tone-dial phone circuits. Pulse-dialing takes longer, but it is cheaper. Tone-dialing is necessary to use alternative long-distance services like MCI or Sprint. Once you get equal access connections in your area, however, you can summon any long-distance carrier with a pulse-dial phone.

• Automatic dial. Several numbers can be stored in the phone's memory and speed-dialed with a couple of digits.

• Screw-in antennas. Most handsets have a small antenna that is pulled out for use, at least toward the fringes of the phone's range. An antenna that screws in is best, because if it breaks off, you can buy a new one and screw it in.

• Extra phone jack. The cordless base station is often installed in a convenient place for a phone. But when the handset is in the rose garden, no one else can use the phone at that location. Some models have a modular jack on the base station for plugging in another phone, which then operates normally.

• Belt hooks. You have to have some way to carry the phone while you are pruning the roses. Some handsets are small enough to slip into your pocket; others have a clip so you can carry them on your belt.

CHAPTER 15 The New Cellular Telephones

Not long ago we went down to the corner of Seventeenth Street and Pennsylvania Avenue in downtown Washington, across the street from the White House, where one of us dialed a number in Salem, Oregon, long-distance. As we walked for several blocks, we talked, holding to our ear a thick telephone handset with a stubby antenna. We kept talking as we rode up several stories on the elevator in an office building. The connection was excellent, just like a regular telephone.

It *was* a telephone, a portable "cellular" radio-telephone. True, at twenty-eight ounces it's a bit heavier than the wrist-radio comic-strip character Dick Tracy made famous. But in the areas where cellular phones are available, you can use them to call any telephone in the world. Detective Tracy surely couldn't do that.

Cellular radio-telephones—available both in cars and as portables—are the newest and hottest wonder of telephony. Now you can finally get a phone installed in your car so you can call your clients, your broker, or your spouse, all the while you are whizzing down the freeway. Or you can reach into your briefcase during lunch, pull out a portable phone, and dial a customer. Even if you don't make a huge sale, your lunchmates will be impressed. General Motors and Ford are offering cellular

"I won't be home for dinner, dear. I'm stuck late at the office."

telephones in some of their luxury cars. Rental agencies are installing cellular phones in portions of their fleets. And in Chicago and Washington, D.C., some taxis have cellular phones so that you can, for a fee, make calls while you are riding.

Cellular telephones spread personal communications far beyond what we're used to. You can work in your car while you are commuting. With a cellular portable or briefcase, you can always be in touch, even if you're sailing on San Francisco Bay or having a meal with friends. Washington attorney George B. Reid, Jr. spends a lot of time talking on the phone to corporate clients. A cellular telephone "makes my car as good as my office for the work I do," Reid said as he talked to us by phone while he drove down the George Washington Parkway. "It allows me to use time that would otherwise be lost. It permits me to return calls the same day rather than the next day." Some of his calls are to Europe. "There's no difference in quality," he said. "It works just like the phone on your desk." One corporate chief executive officer who carries a cellular portable says that if his staff wants to reach him, "they simply call the portable phone. They don't even have to know where I am." This advantage will not be lost on business people.

William McGowan, chairman of MCI Communications Corporation, which has cellular franchises, expects that by the end of the decade every businessman will feel he needs a cellular telephone—except in Los Angeles, where, he says, "everyone will need two, so they can say, 'wait a minute, I've got a call coming in on my other line.' "

Cellular telephones are not yet for everyone. Because they are expensive, from $1000 for a standard car phone to more then $4000 for a portable, plus another $150 a month for service, they are most useful for those whose time is valuable and whose expenses can be written off against their taxes. Professional people, such as doctors, lawyers, real estate developers, contractors, and salesmen, are obvious candidates. Lawyers, for example, can bill clients at the same hourly rate whether they are talking on the phone from their offices or from their cars. Cellular telephone is just starting to be used by giant corporations. Like air-conditioning when it appeared initially, cellular is still regarded as a luxury in most quarters.

First introduced commercially in Chicago in late 1983, cellular telephones will be available in most of the nation's ninety largest metropolitan areas by the end of 1985. These ninety metropolitan areas include about three-fourths of the nation's population. By 1988, there should be cellular service in most of the nation's 305 largest cities.

How Cellular Works

Cellular is likely to be successful because it provides dramatic improvements over historic automobile phones. For years, mobile radio-telephone service was an extremely limited proposition. There were only forty-four radio channels available, and a maximum of about thirty were assigned to any one area. That meant if all thirty channels were occupied—one conversation per channel— and you were the thirty-first mobile phone user who wished to make a call, you had to wait thirty minutes or more, even in a city the size of New York. As you can imagine, mobile radio-telephone service like that could not become very popular. Even with the limited number of channels, long delays in making calls during busy periods, and often poor-quality transmission, there were big waiting lists for mobile service. But with a fully-equipped cellular radio-telephone system, it is possible to make 5000 times as many calls simultaneously in the same metropolitan area, opening up the service to anyone who can pungle up the cash.

That is because cellular radio-telephone systems are technically quite different from traditional mobile telephones. First, the Federal Communications Commission has allocated far more channels to cellular, 666 in all. Second, those 666 channels are broadcast from many different locations. In the old mobile telephone systems, there was one powerful radio station with a large antenna that served an entire city. In the new system, a geographical area is honeycombed with many cells, hence the name "cellular." Each cell has its own low-powered radio transmitter and receiver. As a car with a cellular telephone or a person carrying a portable moves from one cell to the next, the call is transferred automatically. You're unlikely to notice when this transfer takes place, even though your phone is suddenly switched to a different radio station and to another channel while you are talking. It's all done with computers.

Because the cellular signal is low-powered, it doesn't go very far. This permits the same channel you are talking on to be used for calls in other parts of the same metropolitan area without interference. Cellular radio-telephone systems can thus serve a very large number of customers in an area because there are more channels than before—and the larger numbers of channels are reused.

Cellular radio systems are linked to the local telephone exchange. You can call anyone with a cellular phone, just as if you were sitting at your desk at work. You can even call someone who has his own cellular phone. You can sit in a traffic jam on one side of town and call a client who is stopped in his car in another traffic jam on the other side of town.

Unlike local telephone service, which is provided by a monopoly, there is competition in cellular. Two classes of companies are allowed to offer cellular telephone service in every market. One cellular system can be owned by a telephone company, the other by someone else. The two-company rule was adopted by the FCC so that AT&T, which developed cellular, could not monopolize the whole thing.

Cellular telephones come in two basic versions, as car phones and portable phones, with a briefcase hybrid. Car phones are by far the most common, because they are much cheaper. But most believe that, ultimately, portables will be the most popular. Washington Post Company president Richard Simmons, whose company is a partner in several cellular systems, even predicts that by the early 1990s "There will be phones roughly the size of calculators that you carry around in your pocket. They will cost no more than five hundred dollars. They will emancipate people from the necessity of locating a telephone to make calls. The bad news is, you will never be able to get away from the phone—and we'll call it progress."

Car telephones include a small transmitter-receiver unit that is usually mounted in the trunk, an antenna and a control head that includes the handset. In most cellular systems, the telephone touchpad is located on the handset. Many domestic and foreign manufacturers make cellular car phones, but so far only Motorola makes portables, the DYNA T-A-C 8000X and 8000S. Motorola's portables look like a slightly enlarged, somewhat chunky telephone handset, with a stubby antenna at one end.

Portables are less powerful than car units, so they can't be used with some cellular systems. The portable's other limitation is battery life. A portable can listen for calls for about eight hours, but it can transmit for only thirty minutes. After that time it must be charged for a minimum of an hour.

A cellular telephone in a briefcase is a compromise between those who need a phone in their car and those who want a portable, but are not willing to pay high prices for one. One company puts a Panasonic cellular car phone and heavy-duty batteries into a Samsonite briefcase, either black or beige. The company says it is very popular with contractors and realtors who are often out of their offices but are not in their cars. To make a call, you simply open up the briefcase, take out a small antenna, hook it to the top of the briefcase, and dial. There is only one problem with the briefcase phone: it weighs twenty pounds. Try carrying a twenty-pound briefcase from one end of San Francisco

International to the other. The company is working on a lighter model, a spokesman promises.

Manufacturers, too, are working on smaller cellular phones. NEC has a new eight-pound model that looks like a lunch pail. The handset is on the top.

What Cellular Costs

Cellular won't become a truly mass-market item, many experts say, till phone prices drop below $1000. "As prices drop, and they will, the consumers will come in," predicts one industry official. Cellular equipment prices already are falling much faster than anyone dreamed they would. Car phones came on the market at about $3000 or more, plus $200 for installation. Now some units run as low as $1000 plus installation. The Motorola portable, the DYNA T-A-C 8000X, at $3,995, is more expensive. With its own antenna and electrical connection for use in a car, the price is $4,395. Motorola's DYNA T-A-C 8000S has fewer features and costs $2850. The briefcase phone costs $2,495. A plug to power it from the car's cigarette lighter comes with it.

It is not cheap to use a cellular phone, though service charges are dropping sharply. You pay typically $150 to $200 a month in fees, based on the amount of time the phone is used and the time of day. One telephone company, for example, charges forty-five cents a minute during the day and twenty-seven cents a minute off-peak. You are usually charged both for incoming and outgoing calls, though a few systems charge someone who calls your cellular number from a regular telephone. In addition, there is usually some kind of access charge—typically about $35 a month—just to have a cellular phone on the system. Once the call is routed into the telephone system, of course, any message units or long-distance charges are extra.

Some of the best deals are combined rental and service arrangements. Cellular One, a company covering Washington and Baltimore, for example, will install a phone in your car free, and rent it to you for $99 a month, which includes all access charges and one hundred free minutes a month. (This new idea sounds like the old telephone system, doesn't it?) Additional time is charged at forty cents a minute during prime time, twenty-four cents at other periods. After thirty-six months, the $1820 car phone is yours, paid for. A customer can drop out at any time. All he forfeits is his $200 deposit. Marketers say when they started offering cellular service, two-thirds of their customers bought their phones and the rest arranged to lease them. Once the rental plans—which are different from lease plans— were offered, two-thirds of the new customers took them.

It is not hard to find someone to sell you cellular. In any metropolitan area where cellular is offered, the newspapers are filled with cellular ads. The service is usually sold through agents, such as phone stores. They offer a selection of cellular radio-telephones, installation service, and they can sign you up with one of the two local providers of cellular service.

How to Buy

Before you sign up for a phone, be sure to do your homework. Try out a cellular phone. If you can't find a dealer who will let you drive around and talk in his car, rent a car with a phone in it. See if you feel comfortable dialing and changing lanes simultaneously. Talk to several sellers, and look at the deals offered by both system operators in your area. (The second system is not up in many cities yet.) Ask the obvious questions, such as how much each charges per minute, then look at some of the less obvious. Some systems round the time charges to the next higher minute, while some charge by the tenth of the minute, which is much better for the customer. Does the system charge if you try to make a call and the number is busy or doesn't answer? Some do, some don't.

While you may believe that a cellular telephone in your car is just what you need, what about your car? Do you really want a hole for the antenna wire drilled in the center of the trunk lid on your new Mercedes Benz? What happens if you want to sell the car and keep the radio? It is better for reception to drill a hole in the trunk lid or roof of your car. The flat metal of the roof or trunk acts as a "ground plane" for the antenna, engineers say. If drilling a hole in your car is too painful, installers can glue the antenna to the rear window. Performance may suffer slightly, however. If you rent your phone, you are often allowed one free move to another car. After that, you'll pay the regular installation fee.

Like all telephones for sale today, cellular telephones offer many fancy features. Many cellular phones will permit you to store between a dozen and nearly a hundred numbers that can be speed-dialed with a couple of keystrokes, a handy feature when you are trying to call the office and pass someone at the same time. Some features are unique to cellular. If you are out of your car and a call comes in, some models honk the car's horn or flash the headlights. Or they will record the number so you can call it when you return. The provider of the cellular service can enhance the car phone with additional options. The usual numbers you call can be stored in the system's computers. Instead of dialing ten numbers to call your company long-distance, you tap only two.

The cellular phone's calling pattern can be restricted, too, so that it can only receive calls or only make local calls. You can order Call Waiting (a tone on your phone indicating that another call is waiting; hit the hold button to switch to the second call, hit it again to go back to the first). You can make conference calls. Call one number, put it on hold, and call another. Hit the "send" button twice to put everyone on together. Another feature provides that if you don't answer after three rings, your calls are forwarded automatically to another number.

This, of course, is only the beginning of possible cellular features. You can hook a portable computer into a cellular telephone, so you can transmit and receive data right in your car. And you might be able to keep from getting lost. Since the cellular telephone automatically sends out a signal to identify itself whenever it is turned on—even if it isn't being used—the cellular system knows approximately where each phone is located physically. It does this by noting which cell is receiving the phone's signal the strongest. It could be handy to pick up the phone on a dark and stormy night and ask the machine, "Where am I?" A company with a fleet of trucks would always know the location of each of its vehicles. Some cellular telephone manufacturers are working on an auto theft feature. When this becomes available, if someone tries to steal your car, the cellular phone will automatically call the cops, listing the car's license number and location where it is parked.

Roaming with the Phone

Already it is possible to take your cellular phone from your home system and use it elsewhere, a phenomenon known in the business as "roaming." Today you can climb into your cellular-equipped car in Washington, D.C. and talk on the phone continuously till you are well north of Baltimore. As you drive north on the freeway, there is a thirty-minute break in service till you come into range of the Philadelphia cellular system. You can begin making calls from your car again and continue doing so all the way to New York City, except for a five- to ten-minute gap between Trenton and Philadelphia. By the end of 1987, probably sooner, a cellular motorist will be able to travel from well south of Washington to Boston, talking all the way. In the less-populated West, there will be greater gaps. Once the nation's 305 largest cities have cellular, then the FCC is expected to look at systems that will fill in the gaps, such as along major freeways. Eventually, you ought to be able to travel across the country and never be out of range of your cellular radio, so long as you stay on major highways.

Under some roaming agreements between cellular systems you don't even have to give a credit card number. The cellular system will recognize your phone as a roamer from the identification it broadcasts, and will bill your home cellular company for any calls—with a fee for that service, of course. If your cellular system has no roaming agreement with the system you are in, you can pay for calls with a credit card.

If your company operates several vehicles that you plan to equip with cellular telephones, you also ought to look at "specialized mobile radio." This service can be substantially cheaper to operate than cellular if you have three or more vehicles and you need to operate only in a local area. With specialized mobile radio you can contact a dispatcher back at the office—or you can hit a key on the mike and get a telephone dial tone so you can make a phone call. One major difference from cellular is that specialized mobile radio is simpler. That is, you push a key to talk and release it to listen.

Since most cellular users are wheeling down the road while they are talking, some have questioned whether cellular radio promises to be a traffic hazard. How, they ask, can someone give full attention to his driving if he is simultaneously negotiating a deal? Especially if he is holding the phone in one hand and driving with the other. Auto insurance companies, so far, don't seem too worried. They point out that lots of drivers use citizen's band radio and, worse, smoke—and they pay the same insurance rates.

Phoning and Driving

The biggest problem with phoning and driving is that it takes one hand to hold the phone. That is easily remedied with a speakerphone and a microphone (about $200). Cellular One estimates that about 70 percent of their users have speakerphones. The mike is often clipped to the sun visor. Some cellular drivers, however, demand a regular cellular handset so their fellow drivers can see they have a car telephone. To help you phone and drive safely, the editors of *Personal Communications* magazine make these other suggestions:

• Have another passenger place the call for you, if possible.

• Take notes on a small tape recorder, not with pad and pencil.

• Use the memory-dialing function of the phone. If you have a stack of while-you-were-out pink slips of calls to return, enter the numbers into memory before you leave the parking lot. Then you can dial the calls on the road with a couple of keystrokes.

• Learn to operate your phone without looking at it.

• Make sure your phone is mounted where you can reach it easily without moving your body out of position.

• Begin your conversations by telling the other party you are driving. This puts him on notice that you may have to drop the phone to cope with a traffic emergency. It also tells him that you have a car phone.

• Cut your speed while phoning and stay in the right lane.

• Use a car with an automatic transmission. Accelerating with five-on-the-floor while dialing your MCI access number, personal ID, and a long-distance number takes more arms and fingers than most of us possess.

• Keep your calls brief. At forty cents a minute, who needs reminding?

• When you are able to hook your computer to your cellular phone, don't try to make a data call, type on the keyboard, and drive at the same time. Pull over and park to use your computer. That way you won't have to worry about a momentary glitch in the radio signal scrambling your data.

Once you have all that expensive radio telephone gear in your car, do you have to worry all the time that it will be stolen? Probably not, according to insurance company officials. State Farm Mutual, the largest auto insurer, says a cellular radio would be covered by its normal comprehensive policy, with no extra premium. State Farm charges extra to insure CB radios, since they are often stolen. But each cellular radio automatically broadcasts its own identification code and must be "unlocked" by the owner with another digital code. That makes it not much use to a thief or to a potential buyer of hot goods. Still, it makes good sense to unplug the phone from the dash when you park, and stick it in the trunk or your briefcase.

Cellular telephones have the blessing of no less an institution than *The New York Times,* which remarked editorially that "everyone agrees that cellular mobile telephones are a boon." Well, not quite everyone. William Safire, a columnist for the *Times,* drives to work alone in his 1969 Cougar, singing along with Frank Sinatra tapes on the stereo, out of reach of everyone. "Comes the telephone in the car," he writes, "and all that freedom is finished. We will all become always-reachables, under the tyranny of the telephone in the dominion of the dialed. Why do you think they call the mobile phones 'cellular'?"

_____ **TABLE 13** _____

The following thirty largest American cities have cellular telephone service or soon will get it.

New York, Los Angeles, Chicago, Philadelphia, Detroit, Boston, San Francisco, Washington, Dallas, Houston, St. Louis, Miami, Pittsburgh, Baltimore, Minneapolis, Cleveland, Atlanta, San Diego, Denver, Seattle, Milwaukee, Tampa, Cincinnati, Kansas City, Buffalo, Phoenix, San Jose, Indianapolis, New Orleans, Portland.

The FCC has designated the companies that will operate cellular systems in the following sixty cities. Many will begin operation during 1985.

Columbus, Hartford, San Antonio, Rochester, Sacramento, Memphis, Louisville, Providence, Salt Lake City, Dayton, Birmingham, Bridgeport, Norfolk, Albany (NY), Oklahoma City, Nashville, Greensboro (NC), Toledo, New Haven, Honolulu, Jacksonville, Akron, Syracuse, Gary, Worcester, Northeastern Pennsylvania, Tulsa, Allentown, Richmond, Orlando, Charlotte, New Brunswick (NJ), Springfield (IL), Grand Rapids, Omaha, Youngstown, Greenville (SC), Flint, Wilmington, Long Branch (NJ), Raleigh-Durham, West Palm Beach, Oxnard, Fresno, Austin, New Bedford (MA), Tucson, Lansing, Knoxville, Baton Rouge, El Paso, Tacoma, Mobile, Harrisburg, Johnson City (TN), Albuquerque, Canton, Chattanooga, Wichita, Charleston (SC).

CHAPTER 16 Cheap Personal Pagers

Cellular telephones in cars and communicating portable computers in briefcases are wonderful devices to insure that you never go out of touch with your office or home. But what if you don't want to spend $2000 for a cellular telephone or haul a portable computer, light as they are, everywhere you go? Get a pager, and within seconds you can be reached anywhere in a metropolitan area. By the end of 1985, there will be pagers that can reach you in any major city in the nation.

Already nearly four million Americans carry electronic pagers—the familiar "beepers"—in their purses or clipped to their belts, and that number is growing by 20 percent a year. Some experts estimate that by 1990 between ten and twenty million Americans will carry pagers, because they are getting smaller, lighter, cheaper—and much more competent. Some pagers are almost as small as pens.

Pagers are the low-cost alternative in personal communications. A pager in its most elementary form is a device to tell you to call someone. The pager beeps and you know you are supposed to call a certain telephone number. Many young parents who buy pagers regard them as a form of insurance. Paging in many cases is the fastest possible way to get a parent to respond to an emergency at home. Imagine that you are a lawyer and you have a young child at home. You want your babysitter to be able to reach you if there is an emergency, regardless of where you are. If you carry a pager your babysitter can dash to the phone and call your pager's telephone number. Moments later your pager will beep, alerting you to call home. If you are in a conference and don't want the pager to make a noise, you can set it to vibrate instead, although that takes some getting used to. One attorney related that when he first got his vibrating pager, "I'd jump like someone hit me with an electric shock when it went off."

Kinds of Pagers

There are four kinds of pagers, ranging from those that simply beep to those that deliver a short written message on a tiny screen.

Tone-only pagers often cost less than $100 to buy. They can also be leased. Service is an additional $3.50 to $12 a month. Tone-only pagers beep or vibrate if they are called. They can have up to four "addresses," or tones. That means someone carrying a tone-only pager can be alerted to call four different numbers. Tone one means call number A, tone two means call number B, etc. There is usually an additional charge to activate more than one address. The biggest problem with tone-only pagers is that you know someone wants to talk to you, but you don't know who it is.

Voice-and-tone pagers beep, then give you about ten seconds to listen for a broadcast voice message, "Bring home milk and eggs." Voice-and-tone pagers take up a lot of space on radio frequencies, so their numbers are limited. You may not be able to get one in certain large urban areas.

Numeric or digital pagers have a small, calculator-like screen to display numbers, typically phone numbers, although the numbers can be codes you devise. When you get beeped with a numeric pager you know exactly whom you are supposed to call; you don't have to call your home or office first to find out. Numeric pagers cost $150 to $200 or more, depending upon the number of "addresses" the pager can store. They can be leased for $24 to $32 a month, plus service. One large paging service in a competitive market charges $11 a month for service, including one hundred calls. All calls after the one-hundredth in a month cost fifteen cents each.

Alphanumeric pagers are the top of the line. They not only beep, but they can display up to four messages of forty characters each. Advanced alphanumeric pagers soon to come on the market will be able to store and display four messages totaling four hundred characters. A forty-character message could be: CALL CHRIS. MEET CHARLIE FOR LUNCH. You need a communicating personal computer, word processor, or small terminal with keyboard to send messages to an alphanumeric pager. Alphanumeric pagers cost $250 to $400 to purchase, and roughly $30 a month to lease. Service can run $15 a month for a certain number of calls.

It is easy to alert a person wearing a pager. You already know the telephone number of his or her pager. If, for example, you wish to tell the wearer of one of the popular numeric pagers to call someone, you simply dial the telephone number of the pager— which is actually a number at the paging service company. As soon as the phone answers, it beeps. That is your signal to punch the number you wish to send on the phone's touchpad. Then hit the "#" key and your message is on its way. Almost immediately the paging company broadcasts the phone number in digital code by radio to the pager. The pager beeps and the number you tapped into the phone appears on the pager's screen.

The Cost of Paging

Pagers used to be expensive and as a result their use was limited to doctors, repair persons, and those who absolutely had to be in touch with their offices at all times. But now, with pagers getting cheaper and better, the market for them is growing wider every year. At the top end, an alphanumeric pager can be used in an organization for electronic mail. Instead of—or in addition to—

leaving a message in someone's electronic mailbox that he has to remember to look into, you can send a short text message to his pager. He'll be sure to get it. At the other end, some businesses in shopping malls are handing out pagers to their customers. A hair stylist with overflow business, for example, might give a pager to those who want to shop while waiting to be beeped for their turn in the chair. Some husbands of pregnant women carry "baby beepers." When a wife begins labor, she dials her husband's beeper, which means, "come home now."

Consumers are buying inexpensive tone-only pagers to use at home. One company sells a $98 tone-only pager called "Hippo-beepamus," because, of course, you wear it on your hip and it goes "beep." Half its Hippobeepami are beeping in homes, the company reports; the rest are used by small businesses. For example, some parents are hanging tone-only pagers on their small children when they go up the street to visit friends. When the pager beeps, the child knows it is time to come home for dinner. The teenaged daughter in one family always carries a pager when she goes out. That way she can duck into the ladies' room, phone home, and say, "Mom, I've got a skuzzy date." When she rejoins her young man, the beeper suddenly goes off, and, she explains apologetically, that means her parents want her to come right home.

Pagers are available at many outlets. Department stores are starting to carry them. Phone stores sell them, as do most Radio Shack stores. The stores will sell the pager itself; then you must sign up with a company that offers paging services. Usually the retail store can do this for you. You ought to call the companies that offer paging services, because they also sell and rent pagers. You may get a better deal from them. For example, paging companies sometimes sell used pagers that they have been renting to customers. The used pagers may be slightly larger and heavier than the latest models—but they can be a lot cheaper. One company we know sells used pagers, with an excellent warranty, for $29.95 and $39.95. Those deals are very hard to beat.

Pagers are offered by telephone companies and radio common carriers, often the same people who provide mobile radio and cellular radio-telephones. Pager services are usually priced according to the number of calls you receive a month and over how wide an area you wish to be reached. When you shop for a service, ask to have all the various plans explained. If you want to use a pager only for emergencies, you will want a limited service. One company offers tone-only paging for $9 a month with unlimited calls, or $4.95 a month, with each call costing twenty cents. Clearly the second plan is more economical if you receive fewer than twenty calls a month. Some paging companies have extensive radio networks that allow you to range over one or more states. The wider the area over which you wish to be reached, of course, the more you'll pay.

Nationwide Paging

Sometime late in 1985, once the Federal Communications Commission has completed all of its proceedings, paging will go national. You will be able to be paged in any city where a local paging service has signed up with one of the three national paging companies. More than one hundred cities are expected to offer national paging in 1986. If you live in Chicago and travel to Houston, you can tell your Chicago paging company where you are going to be. Then if someone in Chicago pages you, the call will be routed to a satellite earth station in Reston, Virginia. The page will be beamed to a satellite and broadcast back to antennae at local paging companies, including the one at Houston. The Houston company will broadcast the page throughout its area, and your pager will beep. For an extra fee you can be paged throughout the nation. Then you will never be able to escape. Of course, you can always turn your pager off—if you dare.

CHAPTER 17 The Computer-Telephone Connection

F or more people, the telephone hasn't changed significantly since Alexander Graham Bell hollered, "Mr. Watson, come here, I want you!" in that historic first call. They use the phone to send their voices over the wire to distant places. Suddenly, however, it is possible to transmit more than just the dulcet tones from our throats. You can hook a small personal computer to the telephone in order to send and receive digital data. You can combine the wonders of telephony with the wonders of computing. "Nearly every type of computer sold over the next five years will be a potential communications device," says Rudolph Strobl, a senior analyst at the Yankee Group. Indeed, many believe that a combination computer and telephone will eventually be the executive's work station of choice.

Today, anyone with a personal computer—from the simple, inexpensive home computers to the powerful office work stations—can sample the vast riches found at the other end of the wire. You can reach out and grab information from huge commercial data bases that until recently was available only to big corporations and the federal government. You can massage that information in your machine at home in ways that once required mainframe computers. You can use that information to gain a competitive edge in your business or profession, to improve your lifestyle, or simply to make life's tasks a little simpler.

With a communicating personal computer, you can sit at home or in your office and do your banking. You can send and receive electronic letters virtually anywhere at 1200 words per minute. (We flashed chapters of this book back and forth over the phone, between our computers.) You can dig data out of the company's fearsome mainframe computer. You can read the news, research and manage your own stock portfolio, actually buy and sell stocks from home. You can rummage through the libraries of the world, right from your cozy den. You can shop, make an airline reservation, or hold a meeting from home. You can even change your life, if you choose, for you can do some or all of your work at home.

If you own a personal computer, it is not difficult to make it talk on the telephone to virtually any other computer. An Apple can talk to an IBM, a Radio Shack can talk to Kaypro. And all can talk to mainframe computers. You need only two items: a modem and communications software.

Modems

A modem—short for MOdulator-DEModulator—is the "black box" (they come in several colors, actually) that connects your computer to the telephone network. It translates the computer's digital signals to something the telephone system thinks is sound. It converts the computer's zeros and ones into tones and sings them over the wire. At the other end, another modem translates the tones back to digital.

One of our neighbors, a member of the National Academy of Sciences, called one night to say that a relative had given him an inexpensive Commodore 64 computer. "Where can I get a modem for it?" he asked. "Toys'Я'Us," we replied, and for a moment he thought we were kidding. We assured him we were serious. A couple of hours later he called back to say excitedly that he'd bought a modem at the toy store for $60 and that he'd made his first call with it. Modems can cost $600 or more for the fanciest "smart" models. Happily, they are fast coming down in price. Some modems with all the most sophisticated features cost less than $250.

Modems come in two styles, acoustic and direct-connect. Acoustic modems have two cups into which you place the telephone handset, if you are dexterous enough. Unless you plan to spend a lot of time in strange hotel rooms or phone booths, avoid acoustic modems. They are hard to use, they can introduce "noise" into your data, and they can't make calls for you automatically. You want a model that plugs directly into a modular phone jack.

Most popular modems for personal computers operate at one or two data transmission rates, 300 bits per second and 1200 bits per second, also called, incorrectly, 300 baud and 1200 baud. ("Bits" stands for *bi*nary dig*its*. See Chapter 23 for a fuller explanation.) Three hundred bits per second equals 300 baud, but 1200 bits per second equals only 600 baud, a technical bit of trivia useful only for irritating your "computer-literate" friends. Three hundred bits per second roughly equals 300 words per minute, and 1200 bps equals 1200 words per minute. Slower-speed modems are cheaper, but if you ever use a 1200, you'll find a 300, thereafter, to be agonizingly slow. The newest modems can operate at 2400 bps, as well.

Modems can be mounted inside or outside your computer. Internal modems plug into electrical connections or "slots" inside your computer. They are often cheaper than external modems, they are out of sight, they don't require a tangle of wires running around your desk, but they can only be used in the specific machines for which they are designed. External modems, on the other hand, are universal. They plug into the "serial" port of any computer. That's an electrical socket on the computer. You can, for example, move the same external modem from an IBM to an Apple to a Kaypro if you wish. External modems tend to be more costly, however, because you may have to buy a special circuit board (called a "serial card") for your computer in order to be able to plug in your new modem. IBM personal computers and several Apple models, for example, require that you buy a separate serial card, while other computers come equipped from the factory with a serial port, a socket into which you can plug a modem.

Modems can be "smart" or "dumb." With a dumb modem you'll have to dial the phone yourself. Smart modems—the more expensive ones—can remember phone numbers and redial them and perform many other useful tricks, as well. These modems work well with sophisticated software. Although there are many brands of smart modems, you should know that the industry leader is Hayes Microcomputer Products. You'll be able to choose among the widest variety of software that uses modems if you select a modem whose maker claims it is "Hayes-compatible."

Communications Software

Communications software, also called terminal software, enables your computer to talk to other computers and to act together with your modem, screen, disk drives, and printer. Good communications software allows you to capture the text from a computer at the other end of the country and save it to a disk and, at the same time, if you wish, make a copy on your printer. You can transmit data such as text from your machine to another. Some communications programs can make your computer do incredible tricks. One wakes up when you tell it to, say in the middle of the night when the phone rates are low, calls another computer, sends any messages you have stored and picks up any that are waiting on the other computer, says goodnight, hangs up, and then calls the next machine on its list. With such a program—it costs only $100 for each computer—you and your friends or business associates could set up your own computer network and swap data and letters every night, automatically.

Good communications software will eliminate most of the drudgery of computer communications. It will, for example, automate the dreaded "log-on" waltz. When you call a computer information service, such as Dow Jones News/Retrieval, you first dial a local number for a computer network such as GTE Telenet. The computer network answers your call and asks what kind of machine you are using. You reply. Then you are asked to whom you wish to speak. You type in "Dow Jones." Dow Jones answers and asks who you are. You explain, in correct computerese, and Dow Jones asks for your private password. Once you type that, the computer finally lets you in. Whew! Good software will remember all those steps to log into a certain computer. All you have to do is touch a couple of keys to select, say, Dow Jones News/Retrieval, and the computer steps through the log-on waltz, automatically.

Some powerful communications programs for the IBM personal computer (and IBM-compatibles) include Crosstalk XVI from Microstuf, Smartcom II from Hayes, and Personal Communications Manager from IBM. Versions of Crosstalk and Smartcom are also available for the Kaypro. For the Apple II series, ASCII Express from United Software Industries is a high-powered choice. There are also some free or nearly-free communications programs widely used by hobbyists, such as PC-Talk III and PC-Dial for the IBM and Modem7 for machines that use the CP/M operating system. They can be found on computer bulletin boards or acquired through many computer clubs. Satisfied users are sometimes asked, as in the case of PC-Talk III, to send $35 to the writer. It's certainly worth it.

Once you have your computer equipped to talk on the phone, you can plunge into the great electronic beyond. Start at the most elementary level by calling computer bulletin boards. They are electronic versions of the familiar cork-and-thumbtack bulletin boards found at the neighborhood supermarket. Computer bulletin boards are a good place to familiarize yourself with computer communication. They are devoted to every sort of subject from computer hardware to finding a date. Get a list of local bulletin board numbers from a computer store or hobbyist friend. You only really need one number, for most bulletin boards carry a list of numbers for other local boards. The call is free.

Once your computer is connected to a bulletin board, you can read messages left by others and add your own. Many computer clubs run a bulletin board so members can call in with questions. Other members read the questions and reply with help. Some bulletin boards have sections devoted to free software. You can get a new program at the touch of a key. Some of the programs can be very useful, others are merely fun. We once found a free bulletin board program that made our IBM personal computer play blue-grass music.

After you have honed your skill with calls to a few computer bulletin boards, you are ready to tackle most other information services.

Send Electronic Mail

Write a letter to a colleague on your word processor and save the text on a disk. Use your computer software to call an electronic mail service, such as MCI Mail or Western Union's Easylink, and transmit the letter to your colleague's electronic mailbox. He can call the electronic mail service moments later and retrieve the letter, even if he's in another state. Electronic mail is very fast. An electronic note can eliminate "telephone tag." And since most documents these days are composed on a word processor, you can ship a document faster and cheaper by electronic mail than by package express. You can write letters to people who do not have electronic mailboxes, too. MCI Mail, for example, will transmit your letter by wire to a point near your correspondent's home, print the letter on paper, and drop it into the U.S. mail for delivery. Electronic mail costs vary. It costs $18 a year to sign up for MCI Mail, for example. In addition, each 7500-character electronic letter costs $1 to send, nothing to receive. Letters that are mailed cost the sender $2. They can cost up to $25 to be delivered by courier. At present, electronic mail correspondents must all subscribe to the same service in order to communicate. MCI has announced MCI Mail Link to connect MCI Mail to other electronic mail networks that were previously incompatible.

Telecommute

Be "in" the office wherever you are, as long as you have a communicating personal computer and a phone line handy. This newfound power can change the way you live and work. Before we got computers, we used to stay at work late at night to finish magazine stories. Now we go home at the regular hour, have dinner with our families, and continue working on our machines at home. When we're through, we send our stuff over the telephone to *Newsweek*'s computer and go to bed.

When we travel, we pack an inexpensive, four-pound, battery-operated portable computer. We can write stories on an airplane. When we get to the airport, we do our Superman number. We dive into a phone booth, whip out our computer, and send off our story. One traveling executive told us, "I can be in my office when I'm not in my office." Not only that, he said, "I can write a memo and send it to five, ten, a hundred people. I can appear to be all over the place."

Professional women with new babies may be able to continue working at home with communicating computers linking them to their offices.

You needn't be a frequent traveler or a new mother to enjoy the change a communicating personal computer can bring to your life. The machine raises the concept of flexible work hours to an entirely new level. Groups of workers, such as computer programmers who often work through the night, can exchange messages and programs from their homes at any time. All this power can change the way we live. An executive at the leading edge of the information revolution told us, "When you have a tube in your office and a tube at home, your workday can become extremely undisciplined. Sometimes when I get up for a potty call at 3 A.M., I'll sign in to see if I have any messages." Soon, he discovers, he's worked an hour or two at his terminal in the middle of the night. What is really weird, he said, is that he gets replies to some of the messages he sends out in the middle of the night—before he returns to bed. Other "white worms," as he calls them, are out there working, too.

Search Through the Company's Mainframe Computer

Touch a key or two on your personal computer and call up data from deep in the bowels of your company's mainframe. Store the data in your own machine, manipulate it, use it. You can do that while sitting at your desk in the office—or anywhere you have a phone and a personal computer. The professionals in the data processing department will not like you.

Invest

Call Dow Jones News/Retrieval in the evening, touch a couple of keys, and get five of the day's closing stock quotes, for fifteen cents. Not surprisingly, investors are among the biggest users of communicating personal computers. They can get stock quotes, company filings with the federal government, even weather and movie reviews, using their regular communications programs. Or, using special financial software, an investor's computer can call the service and get reams of historical information on certain stocks. After hanging up, the investor can have his machine draw many different colored charts so that he can do a technical analysis of the stocks to try to figure out when to buy or sell. If he prefers to do fundamental analysis of stocks, he can do that, too. Some new services allow investors to use their personal computers to place buy and sell orders with their brokerage houses. This is bad news for your broker.

Bank

Dial up your bank, ask for your checking account statement, and read it on your computer screen. Home banking services are just getting started, but they promise to grow large. Studies show that over 60 percent of the first-class mail that leaves a private residence contains a check to pay a bill. All this could be replaced by electronic banking. One of us banks in Memphis, although he lives in Virginia. His employer deposits his paycheck in the Memphis bank—electronically, of course. He's given the bank a list of twenty-three merchants with whom he normally does business, including the paperboy, the orthodontist, the electric company, and all credit card companies. Whenever he gets a bill, such as for a credit card, he simply calls the bank with his computer. From the list of twenty-three companies displayed on his screen, he selects the credit card company, types in the amount to pay and the day on which it is to be paid. The bank charges twenty cents a bill, the same as the first-class stamp we used to put on the return envelope.

Reserve Flights

Ask your computer how to get to Chicago, and how much it will cost. The Official Airline Guide is available online through CompuServe, The Source, Dow Jones News/Retrieval, and directly from the company. You can find all the flights, direct and connecting, from where you are, to where you want to be. Once you've picked a flight, you can display all the fares available and what you have to do to qualify for the cheap ones. That's not all. TWA has made its reservations system available to the general public on CompuServe, so you can book the flight after you've picked it out. Your travel agent will go wild when he hears you can do that.

Read the News

Turn on your computer to find out what is happening in the U.S. Senate—or to your university football team. The Associated Press, United Press International, Dow Jones News Service, and other more specialized news services, are available from several different information services, including CompuServe, The Source, Dow Jones News/Retrieval, Delphi, ITT Dialcom, and others. You can search the news files by key words—such as "Joe Montana"—so you get only those stories that interest you. Electronic editions of some newspapers, such as the *Washington Post*, are available daily.

Search Through Libraries

Rummage through the libraries of the world without leaving your study. There are more than 2000 data bases that you can sign up to use, from the Academic American Encyclopedia to the Zoological Record. A data base is a collection of information, like a library or a newspaper's clipping file, that can be searched and read by computer. Data bases can contain abstracts of articles, the full text of the articles, or series of numbers, such as Wyoming oil production-by-month. Major data base vendors include Dialog Information Services, the biggest, with 200 data bases; Bibliographic Retrieval Services; and System Development Corporation Information Services. Dialog will even let you search through all the nation's Electronic Yellow Pages. Can you imagine the customer list you could generate from that!

While most data bases are used by universities, large corporations, and the federal government, data base vendors are now busily courting individuals with personal computers. Dialog and

BRS, for example, both offer a set of their most popular data bases that consumers can use at reduced rates on evenings and weekends. Both bill you by credit card (Dialog's Knowledge Index is $24 an hour, counted by the minute; BRS After Dark is comparable). Although most of the data is stored as article abstracts, not full text, the abstracts often contain all the relevant information you need. For anyone who has to write a report on a strange topic, access to a service like Dialog can be invaluable. Students, especially, would find the services useful. A quick romp through the electronic files would provide a spectacular, up-to-date bibliography for a major paper. Medical people can find an endless array of valuable online services. Other professionals, such as lawyers, regard online services such as Westlaw and Lexis as better and faster than a law library. It won't be long before the law books in an attorney's office are there only for show. All the real research will be done online.

Hold a Computer Conference

Call a meeting on your computer. Get all the experts in your club or company together—regardless of where they happen to be physically—to produce a major report. You could do it in the traditional way by having them all gather, expensively, in one place to meet face-to-face. Or you could hold a computer conference, with each expert at his own terminal. Computer conferencing is a kind of glorified electronic mail. Meetings begin when the chairman sets out a topic to be discussed or a task to be accomplished. This is done online. Then all invited participants call the central computer, on which the meeting is held, to read what the chairman has said. They review his comments and those of others. Then they add their own. The conferees don't type back and forth at each other—that would be chaos. Rather, each participates according to his own schedule. Some can call early in the morning, others will take a free moment during the day to check in. The chairman guides the discussion and summarizes thoughts. He conducts balloting on some issues. He may arrange for one or more people to draft conclusions for the group.

Obvious advantages to computer conferencing include no time or geographic restrictions. No one is ever late for a meeting. No one has to play telephone tag. There is no expensive travel, no waiting at the airport. Everyone can print and keep a copy of all that has been said. Responses can be better considered. The quality of the meeting can be higher, because more of those you really want can join the group. A final report is easier to write because everyone's comments are available to read.

There are also disadvantages. Text scrolling up a video screen cannot convey the nuances of speech or the skeptical arch of an eyebrow. Electronic dialog can drift if it isn't closely monitored. Those who can't type or spell well may be intimidated, although they could dictate their comments to a secretary if they wished.

Computer conferencing is just getting started. The most popular conferencing system, called Participate, is available through The Source, ITT Dialcom, and other computer information services.

Publish

Set type for your church bulletin, newsletter, or novel from the privacy of your home. Many printing companies now let you send text from your computer to theirs over the telephone. They can then set the type in a jiffy. They don't have to retype all your copy—so any mistakes are yours alone.

Shop

Browse through 50,000 items at Comp-U-Store, seven days a week, twenty-four hours a day, and save, it is claimed, up to 40 percent on what you buy. Comp-U-Store is available direct or through CompuServe, Dow Jones News/Retrieval, and The Source. The best use of Comp-U-Store is comparison shopping. Pick out what you want to buy and check the prices on the tube.

That way you'll know if you're getting a good price for a stereo or a microwave oven from your local discounter. If it turns out that you can save a lot with video shopping, you can place your order online. Unfortunately, the goods you order are not delivered electronically. They usually come by truck.

Meet Your Friends

Travel to a common ground at the confluence of the telephone system and a mainframe computer. There you can meet people with interests similar to yours. Do you want to discuss the problems of your IBM personal computer? Join the IBM users' group on CompuServe or post a message on the IBM bulletin board on The Source. Ask a question and you'll soon get an expert answer from someone—maybe on the other side of the continent—who has had the same problem before. Special Interest Groups—SIGs in the jargon—range from antiques to Zenith. On the way from A to Z you'll pass such delights as Veterinarians' Forum, where you can take up your pet subjects. If you're sufficiently daring, you can try the simulated Citizens Band on CompuServe. You assume a CB handle, a phony name, jump in, and start typing, all in real time. It's truly a wonder of the computer age. You can type back and forth to someone you don't know, who can't spell, who lives in a part of the country you wouldn't visit if you could, on subjects you may not care about. You may be asked by someone with a name like Conan the Librarian to go off on a separate channel to talk privately. People seem to love it.

Executive Work Stations

You can get all this wonderful stuff on your personal computer today, right from your home or office. It's not hard to do now, and it's going to get even easier. Many manufacturers are starting to build combination computer-phone executive work stations. The work station typically includes a computer (often IBM-compatible), telephone, calendar, scratch pad, and lists of phone numbers. That way you can sit at your desk, call your video Rolodex onto the computer screen, page through it, and pick a number to call. Your computer will place the call, of course. It's the same with any information service. Look at the list and tell the computer to make the call. Meanwhile you can check your personal calendar. You can also use the machine to do all of the usual computer tasks such as word processing, financial management, data base management, and games.

You don't need a special combination computer phone-work station to do all this. You can use a regular personal computer and jazz it up with a few simple, inexpensive programs. If you have an IBM personal computer with a modem, for example, you can give it just about all the features of a computer phone with about $200 worth of programs to manage your phone lists, to dial your phone numbers, to call information services, to keep your calendar, even to give you an alarm clock and calculator on your screen at the quick touch of two keys. Several software companies make programs to do this.

If we're typing away on our word processor and we want to make a phone call, we simply hit a couple of keys to call up our list of phone numbers. We select a number by running the cursor to it, then hit another key to dial the number. When the party answers, we can pick up the phone and talk as always.

18 Controlling Your Home by Phone: Protect Life, Health, Property

*Y*ou're an older person and you live alone. What happens if you fall and can't get up? Who will help you?

You're at a party and a burglar breaks down your back door. Who will call the police?

You're away on vacation and the pipes freeze and break, flooding your basement. Who will shut off the water? Who will call the plumber?

You'll be home in a hour and you want the furnace turned on so the house will be warm when you get there. Who will turn on the heat?

We really asked the questions wrong. We should have asked "what" rather than "who" would help you. In all these cases—and in many others, as well—your telephone can get you the help you need, automatically. Telephones and devices you can connect to the telephone line are now "smart" enough to call the police or fire departments, turn the heat up when you tell them to, check to make sure the electricity is working, or summon help when you need it. These devices, furthermore, are not very expensive. They can pay for themselves easily by providing peace of mind. And if they are ever actually needed, they pay for themselves many times over. Beyond providing emergency help, home control by telephone can make your life more enjoyable—or, at least, more efficient.

What we're really talking about here is more than safety, security, and protection of property. It is now possible to run virtually your entire home by remote control. No matter where you are, your telephone line can link you to virtually every electrical device in your home. Even if you don't worry about fire or burglars, you may love to have the ability to turn your porch lights on and off from a pay phone, to leave messages that show up on your television set, or start your air-conditioner in Atlanta just before you get on the plane in Seattle. Home control by phone has only recently become practical, and consumer surveys show that people now are as interested in it as they were in home video in the late 1970s. It will become at least as popular as home video, we believe, for home control by phone can provide more freedom—as well as more security—for today's busy families.

Emergency-call systems plug into an electrical outlet and a modular telephone jack. They work with different kinds of sensors, depending on the emergency you wish to deal with. While there are several different possible systems, here we will describe the versions offered by AT&T through their Phone Centers. They consist of a programmable console that costs $200 to $250 and sensors that cost $30 to $50. The sensors transmit to the console by radio. To protect against fire, you install a small fire sensor (it's slightly larger than a hockey puck) on the ceiling next to your present smoke detector. If your smoke detector goes off, the sensor "hears" the sound and sends a radio message to the emergency-call system elsewhere in the house. The emergency-call system shouts, "Fire! Fire! Fire!" for thirty seconds through its built-in speaker. If someone is home, he's probably already heard the smoke detector go off and has taken the burned toast out of the toaster. He can hit the cancel button to make the emergency-call system shut up and go back on alert.

If no one cancels the emergency call, the system dials one of two numbers you have programmed into the emergency-call console. The first number may be the fire department. When the fire dispatcher answers, the system hollers in a synthetic voice, "There is a fire" at a certain address. The voice tells the person who answered that if he understands the message to press "3" on the phone's number pad. If the number is pressed, the system assumes that help is on the way. But if the person who answered the phone does nothing, the system assumes that he didn't understand. It then tries a second phone number you have programmed, perhaps your own number at work or that of a neighbor who is usually at home. It will try the numbers alternatively for half an hour before giving up.

If no one is home when a fire breaks out, it could burn for a long time before someone sees it and calls the fire department. You can imagine how much faster help can be summoned if you have an emergency-call system that dials the fire department the moment the smoke alarm goes off. If you do have a fire, quick response by the fire department could limit the damage. Fireman's Fund, a large insurance company, thinks so highly of the emergency-call system that the company gives a 5 percent credit on homeowners' insurance (which includes fire insurance) to those who have installed it. The average annual premium for homeowners' insurance is roughly $300 a year, so you could save $15 a year. That's not to say anything of the piece of mind such a device could bring you.

Think about how useful this emergency-call system would be for a remote cabin or condominium that often stands idle for days or weeks at a time. If a fire breaks out, the system calls the fire department, automatically. The same kind of system can monitor the temperature at your mountain cabin (or home), check whether the electricity is working, and let you know if water rises to abnormal levels. If, for example, the heat goes off in winter, a sensor will alert the emergency-call system that the temperature in the house is dangerously low (you set the temperature at which you wish to be alerted). The system works exactly like the fire alert. It tries to call two pre-programmed numbers to announce that "there is an emergency."

These sensors can be used in many different situations. If you are a butcher or grocer, for example, you may want to have the emergency system call you if the electricity goes off so you can protect the food in your freezers. If you live in an area that has severe rain storms, you will want to have the system call you if the basement begins to flood.

Emergency-call systems are especially useful for the elderly or the infirm. An older person who lives alone may not be able to get anyone to come to his aid if he should fall or have some other emergency. Help can always be near if he carries a medical-alert transmitter. It is a small device that can be worn around the neck on a lanyard or clipped to a belt. If someone needs help, he simply pushes a button on the transmitter. That radios the emergency-call system, which dials the first of two programmed numbers to say there is an emergency at a certain address. The number could be that of a nearby relative or a neighbor.

If you don't have a relative nearby who can come help ninety-year-old Aunt Nettie, you can have the first call be made to a security service that is in the business of monitoring calls and alarms. The security service will receive the synthetic voice call from the emergency-call system in Aunt Nettie's home. The dispatcher on duty will pull Aunt Nettie's file to see what he is supposed to do. The security service will always answer the phone, and they can try to reach you, Aunt Nettie's neighbor, the fire department's rescue squad, or anyone else you tell them to until they get results. The call monitoring service should cost $20 to $30 a month. Some hospitals are starting to use medical-alert calling systems with their outpatients. If a patient who is at home has a severe problem and can't get to the telephone, he hits the button and the hospital staff knows that it should respond. (While this is a nice humanitarian touch, many hospitals see the service as a marketing device for attracting patients in an increasingly competitive medical market.)

You can also get systems that will alert you or the police or anyone else you designate if someone is trying to break into your house. They have been around for a long time, but microelectronics are making them cheaper and more effective. A full-featured security system sufficient for a condominium may cost $700 while a system for a detached house could cost $1000. These systems will go off if someone breaks down a door or window. Sensors, using ultrasound, detect motion while others detect body heat to tell if someone is in the house. (They can also detect the presence of the family Dalmatian, so they're not useful for people with pets.) The systems can sound a local siren or other warning and also call the police or the security service dispatcher. When the dispatcher gets a call from the system, he responds as necessary. The police he sends may find the door broken down. The dispatcher looks in your file to find whom you've requested to have fix a broken door or window if you can't be located.

Security systems are sufficiently complicated that you may want to get an expert to install them. You will find the Yellow Pages of the telephone book filled with ads for security services. You'd be well advised to pick one of the few that have met the Underwriter's Laboratory standards for central station services. A service that has met the UL standards is more likely to still be in business when your emergency call does go through.

Unfortunately, no one has invented an emergency-calling system yet that has a fail-safe against false alarms, although some come close. One of us can remember two policemen rushing up to a neighbor's house with their handguns drawn. They found, to their disgust, that the neighbor's burglar alarm had inadvertently sent a false alarm to the police station. Because of this, most local governments charge a fee for a false fire or police alarm. You should ask the authorities in your area what their policy is.

Besides summoning help automatically when sensors detect trouble, your phone can also link you to the electrical devices in your home, so you can control them from afar. Home computerists have been able to do this for some time. They call their personal computers by phone and get the computer to turn something on or off. Now the big appliance companies are starting to look at this new capability. General Electric, for example, makes a device called the HomeMinder System that connects your phone, television set, and appliances. With HomeMinder, you can call home and turn any 120-volt appliance on or off, control the furnace and air-conditioner, and leave messages that can be read on the television screen.

You can, for example, call HomeMinder from work to turn on the front porch lights. Install a HomeMinder switch on the porch lights' circuit. HomeMinder lets the phone ring eight or nine times before it answers. That's so that if someone else is home, he or she can pick up the phone first. If no one else is there, once the machine answers, you tap codes on the telephone's touch-tone pad, instructing the machine to turn on the porch lights.

The system sends its signals over the house electric circuits to modules that actually do the work. When they detect a command coming over the electric circuit, the modules turn light switches and appliances on and off, and even control the furnace. The furnace control is especially clever. Under your regular home thermostat you attach a small pad which is connected to the HomeMinder. The pad can be heated slightly, to fool the thermostat. It turns the furnace off by heating the pad so the thermostat thinks the room is 15 degrees warmer than it really is. Thus, if the thermostat is set to keep the room at 65 degrees and HomeMinder has instructed it to turn off (by heating the pad), it will allow the room temperature to drop to 50 degrees before the furnace turns on again. The same scheme is used in reverse to control the air-conditioner. If you want to keep your house at 75 degrees in the summer, you set the thermostat to 90. When the pad under the thermostat is heated, the thermostat thinks it has to cool the room. When the pad is off, the thermostat won't turn the air-conditioner on till the air temperature in the room with the thermostat reaches 90 degrees.

You can program the HomeMinder to operate the appliances throughout your house. During the winter, the HomeMinder can be set to turn the furnace on at 6:30 A.M., off at 7:30 A.M., on again at 5:30 P.M. and off at 10 P.M. Meanwhile, the lights can be dancing to a different tune. To change that schedule, all you have to do is call the system by phone.

You can also call HomeMinder and leave two messages. One says that you will be home at a certain time. The second says that you can be reached at a certain number. You call the system from any touch-tone phone and leave the messages by hitting the appropriate keys on the phone's number pad. The person at home can display the messages by turning on the television set. When you leave for a few days, you can put the HomeMinder into its security mode. It turns lights and radios on and off throughout the house at random, to give the place a "lived-in" look to any would-be burglar.

HomeMinder is not cheap. It can be purchased with a top-of-the-line, twenty-five-inch GE television set for about $1300, including a lamp- and an appliance-control module. If you already have a satisfactory television set, you can buy the main HomeMinder controller and two modules for between $370 and $390. Each additional module is $20 to $30, and you can hook as many as a hundred of them to a single controller.

Emergency-call systems and home-control systems can give you much more control over your home and life. You needn't have quite so much fear that when you return after a long trip you'll find your house burned to the ground, ransacked, or all the meat in the freezer spoiled because the power went off. While you are away, you can be assured that a faithful machine with battery backup will call for help if it is needed. And you can be comforted by the knowledge that an older relative is always able to call for assistance.

CHAPTER 19 800 and 900 Numbers

Remember Rod Serling, and how he used to say, "You unlock this door with the key of imagination. Beyond it is another dimension—a dimension of sound, a dimension of sight, a dimension of mind. You've just crossed over into the twilight zone"? We're always reminded of Serling when we think about the world of 800 and 900 telephone numbers.

800 and 900 numbers are the gateways to a special information world in which you can buy a mink coat, make a Hawaiian hotel reservation, or inquire about a personal computer three thousand miles away, without having to pay for a long-distance call. You can dial up the plot of your favorite soap opera and check the score of your favorite football team whenever you feel like it.

800 numbers are the special toll-free numbers that businesses lease from AT&T so that out-of-town customers can call them with orders or inquiries and have the calls billed to the companies' accounts. The series is also known as 1-800 numbers because some local telephone systems require that you dial "1" first. Just look in your local newspaper or favorite magazine, and you will probably find several advertisements listing an 800 number to call for further information.

If you're not planning to make a trip and have no interest in purchasing goods over the phone, but are looking for a way to inform or entertain yourself, 900 numbers may be just your thing. Unlike 800 calls, which you can make for free, you must pay a small charge to call a 900 number. At the other end of the line lies the latest stock-market news, horoscopes, and even sexual messages, should you be so inclined.

So many businesses have 800 numbers that AT&T has a directory-assistance number and special phone books just for the 800 series. Say you want to visit the Williamsburg Inn in Colonial Williamsburg, Virginia. If you knew the area code for Williamsburg, you could call ordinary long-distance directory assistance there for the hotel reservations number, and then spend more time and money calling the number provided by the phone company to request reservations. Or, you could call 800-555-1212, which is AT&T's toll-free directory-assistance number for 800 services, and ask if the hotel has an 800 number for you. On receiving that number, you could phone the inn to set up your vacation plans without spending a nickel of your own money.

The 800 service phone books are a great guide to a never-never world where phone calls to just about anywhere are free. The seventy-eight-page consumer edition ($6.25) has two sections: a 236-page topical listing, like the Yellow Pages, and an alphabetical listing by company. For each listing, there's a little note telling you if there are any restrictions on use of the number. For example, to call the Popcorn Factory in Lake Forest, Illinois, you can call 800-228-5000, from anywhere in the country except Alaska, Hawaii, or Illinois. The notation shows up in the directory as "(US EX AK, HI, IL)." The topics cover the range from "Accountants—Certified Public," to "Wine & Spirits." Along the way, you'll find listings for gourmet foods, hotels (one of the largest sections), motion picture film libraries, satellite equipment and services, telephone companies (MCI obviously believes in the service—it has a big ad), tourist bureaus and travel. In some cases, you'll meet companies that don't think just any phone number will do. Gallery One, of San Francisco, Los Angeles, Barcelona, and Paris, makes sure you'll remember it when you call 800-342-5278. Its number spells 800-FINE-ART.

To order the 800 Directory, call 800-242-4634. It's toll-free, of course. Should you be interested, there's also a directory for

small-business persons, which costs $8.75. The business direc-
tory includes numbers for many wholesalers selling basic office
supplies. Included in the directories is a cut-out card that you
can send in to AT&T to determine if you "qualify" for a free
copy of next year's directory.

The 900 series doesn't have its own phone book, but if you
want to know what 900 services AT&T is offering on a particular
day, just dial (1)-900-555-1212 (again, it's free). The New Tri-
viology Trivia Quiz is one of your options. So is the American
Cancer Society's message on the evils of cancer. Interested in
what the savings and loan lobby is doing in order to better life in
the United States? Listen to the U.S. League of Savings Washington Phone Report. Sports fans, of course, are big customers.
Two sports services, National Sports Scores and the J.K.
Sports Wire will keep you current. If you want to set your watch
as precisely as possible, phone the Naval Observatory Report.
Its clock is the most accurate around. When the space shuttle is
flying, you can call NASA's Dial-a-Shuttle, which allows you to
listen in to what the astronauts are saying in orbit.

As we warned earlier, 900 calls don't come for free, unfortunately. If the number you are calling begins 900-410-XXXX, it
costs fifty cents for the first minute, plus thirty-five cents for
every minute thereafter, plus tax. Calls whose second three
digits are 976 (sports scores, for example), 210, 720, or 407 are a
flat fifty cents per call, plus tax.

Another 900 series that can be fun to use is AT&T's polling
service. For fifty cents per call, plus tax, this service gives you
the opportunity to vote on some of the weightiest and silliest
questions ever put to the American public. Last year, for
instance, Purina Dog Chow ran a television promotion to pick
the "Great American Dog," complete with pictures of five of the
cutest doggies you ever did see. To vote for Bandit, Buddy,
Dixie, Geena, or Misty (and owners), all you had to do was dial
1-900-720- and the particular number assigned to one of the five
choices.

Many local telephone companies offer service similar to
AT&T's 900 series, where subscribers can call up and hear
information over the telephone. The local services are called
976 numbers because of the three digits with which they begin.
In some places they are also referred to as "Dial-It" numbers.

The charges for these calls typically range from fifty cents to one dollar and are billed to your local phone number.

Until 1983, the local phone companies had complete responsibility for 976 numbers and oversaw every aspect of their operation, from setting up the lines to making the tapes for callers. But the FCC ruled that local telephone companies shouldn't do anything more than install the lines, so the programming was taken out of the local telephone company's control. Different companies handled the matter in different ways. In Chicago, when Illinois Bell was forced to give up the 976 service, it took sealed bids and awarded the 976 franchise to one company, Phone Programs Illinois. In January 1983, when the transfer occurred, there were only three 976 services in Chicago—time, weather, and sports. The system is now at capacity with eighteen lines and a network capable of handling three thousand simultaneous calls in the Chicago area. New York Telephone awards its 976 circuits by lottery. Late last year they had forty-three lines running and scores of applicants waiting for a chance to get one.

Losing control of the programming has been a headache for New York Telephone because of the infamous Dial-a-Porn service. The service, sponsored by the publishers of *High Society* magazine and featuring seductive female voices offering sexually explicit messages, is the most popular dial-it service in history.

Dial-a-Porn received 800,000 calls per day in May 1983, and 180 million calls in the year ending February 1984. That's pretty heavy breathing, even for a service that has the capacity to receive 50,000 calls per hour. By comparison, the second most popular service, horse race results, received only 29 million calls per year. While 80 percent of the Dial-a-Porn calls were from New York, many were from out-of-state. Both Pentagon and Congressional offices were represented.

In 1984 the FCC made an attempt to curb the Dial-a-Porn programming by restricting it to nighttime hours and limiting payment to credit cards. But a federal appellate court in New York threw out the FCC's rules on constitutional grounds. The FCC is looking for a new way to regulate these services, but meanwhile, Dial-a-Porn services are spreading to other cities across the U.S.

_____ **TABLE 14** _____
Dial-up Sampler

Here are some listings from the 800-world. These numbers are subject to change.

800-CHEER-UP	Nationwide Gift Liquor
800-FOR-CARS	Thrifty Rent-a-car
800-BALLYS-7	Bally's Casino
800-NEIMANS	Neiman-Marcus
800-FLOWERS	national florist number
800-DATAGEN	Data General computers
800-BE-SHARP	Sharp computers
800-GO-U-HAUL	U-Haul rentals
800-44PUPPY	Puppy Chow Guide
800-HOTELS-1	Stouffer Hotels

If you were curious about the national 900-numbers in service, and had called the national 900-information number, 900-555-1212, last year, here's what you would have found:

Santa	900-40-SANTA(407-2682)
National Sports	900-976-1313
U.S. League of Savings Associations	900-210-8900
Naval Observatory Master Clock	900-410-TIME(8463)
J.K. Sports Wire	900-410-3300
Cardholders bargain line	900-410-4000

In New York, for example, there's a wider variety of calls possible on the local dial-it service. Here's a sampler:

212-976-2020	lottery results
212-976-3636	fairy tales
212-976-3838	Dial-a-Joke
212-976-4141	Dow Jones
212-976-5050, 5454, 5656, 6262	horoscopes
212-976-6363	Dial-a-Soap

In Chicago:
312-976-1313   sports

In Philadelphia:
215-976-8383   One Life to Live (soap
                                       opera)
215-976-5233   Dial-a-Joke

6

Small Business
Telephone Survival

CHAPTER 20 Phones for Small Business

A Greek-American photographer we know once said that you will know when you've reached adulthood when you look around the table on a big holiday and there's no one else to do the carving. Much the same can be said about the small business person.

You won't find many statues honoring the corner grocer or the local manufacturer, but small business people built the American economy. Of the more than 17 million businesses in this country, over 99 percent have fewer than one hundred employees, and study after study shows that when it comes to creating jobs, the small business person contributes far more than the huge Fortune 500 companies. Nevertheless, when it comes to economic policy-making, small businesses always seem to be ignored. While the big companies have the money and power to command the politicians' attention, and consumers can usually count on public interest groups and liberal politicians to defend their interests, the small businessman almost always has to carve the turkey himself if he wants to eat. Of all the messes that the politicians, judges, and bureaucrats have left the small business person to cope with on his own, the dismantling of the phone system has to rank among the worst.

We're not suggesting, of course, that the small business community is the only one to find the post-divestiture era confusing. But to a great many small enterprises, the telephone is third only to salaries and rent as a cost of doing business. Failure to master the ground rules of the new telephone game could be a matter of economic life or death. Managed properly, your company's phone system can serve as a strategic asset to enhance productivity, improve competitiveness and generate new revenue. If not dealt with carefully, you may mishandle calls from customers or suppliers that you can ill-afford to lose.

As a small business, you don't have the luxury of keeping telecommunications managers on your payroll the way the Fortune 500 companies do, or of hiring consultants to deal with the confusion as might a company with a thousand employees. A book like this isn't going to solve all your telephone problems either. But we can show you how to evaluate your situation and suggest the kinds of questions you'll need to ask if you are going to find your way through the telephone wilderness. Since 95 percent of small businesses have six telephone lines or fewer, our advice is geared especially to your circumstances.

The problem before you breaks down into two issues: what kind of equipment to buy or lease, and what kind of local and long-distance service options to subscribe to. For many of you, the selection of local and long-distance service plans won't require much attention. According to a recent study by the National Federation of Independent Business, only a third of small business calling is long-distance, and of that, the vast majority is intrastate. Because of this, long-distance bills are not likely to be of great concern. On the local service side, the only option available to businesses today in many states is measured service, in which you pay by the number of calls you make and the amount of time you use. Even if you wanted to, you couldn't choose a local service option.

Where equipment is concerned, choices abound, however. Because it's often difficult to understand the technologies involved, and the size of the investment required is large, the mission is complicated. In this chapter we will describe what the leading equipment options are for a small business. We will follow this with chapters on how to shop for a system of your own, and on specialized business service options available to aid your company.

The Single-Line Telephone

Research by the National Federation of Independent Business shows that 39 percent of all businesses have only one telephone line. In most of these cases, that's smart. If you work by yourself, or have a business that doesn't require much telephoning, there's no point in paying for equipment and service that you won't use. Before jumping to the conclusion that you need more than one line, you should ask yourself whether your requirements can't be met by adding an extension phone or two to your first line, or by getting yourself an answering machine (Chapter 13) or employing an answering service when you can't pick up the phone yourself. Using a cordless phone as an extension can be a fine idea at times. While you run the risk of electronic eavesdropping (see Chapter 14), being able to carry the phone from room to room can be both convenient and cost-effective. Don't forget, local rates for business lines are often three or four times that of residential service.

As we showed in our chapters on residential equipment and service, many of the calling features that previously were associated only with office systems are available to single-line users today. Thanks to modern electronics, there are many single-line phones with speed-dialing, automatic redial, hold buttons, and built-in speakers. In addition, the local phone company will provide both Call Waiting and three-way conferencing at relatively modest monthly charges.

Two-Line Telephones

One of the first principles of business is that you often have to spend money to make money. A two-line phone can be one of the most productive investments a small business can make. If you work by yourself, a two-line phone allows you to put a call on hold while you dial a second person to check on something. At the touch of a button all three of you can talk together. Even better, a two-line phone enables you to have more than one person in your office making or receiving calls at the same time, provided there's another phone or extension that's wired for the second line. Since a second business line often costs significantly less than your first one, it may not even be that expensive.

There are two types of two-line phones, the electromechanical and the electronic, or as some cognoscenti put it, the old kind and the new kind. Both provide access to two lines from the same phone, but use different methods to shut off the second line while you are talking on the first. In the older electromechanical models, there is a knob you turn to designate the line you wish to use, and a switch to place a call on hold. The "hold" is accomplished by mechanically "short-circuiting" the line that you wish to leave for a moment. Because of the way the hold-feature works, it is not possible to take a call on one line, put it on hold, and transfer the call to a second phone.

This is not the case with electronic two-line phones, which allow you to transfer calls that have been put on hold without difficulty. As another benefit, the electronic phones use buttons with lights to signal when a call is coming in or a line is occupied.

Key Systems

The familiar six-button phone that we've all seen in offices is called a "key set" in the telephone industry. When several key sets are used together in an office, they're known as a "key system." First introduced by Bell in 1925, the key set made it possible for the business person to have several different lines at his disposal without having on his desk a different phone for each. On a key phone, each button, or key, connects you with a different line. With over 28 million key sets in service at last count, they are the mainstay of small-business telephone systems today.

Key sets come in both electromechanical and electronic versions. The electromechanical key systems, or "1A2 systems" as they are referred to in the industry, are virtually indestructible. Should you outgrow your phone network, 1A2 systems can also be expanded to accommodate fifty to one hundred phone lines.

1A2s have their drawbacks, however. Because they are electromechanical instruments, they are packed with switches and relays that run on electricity. This requires that there be costly separate copper circuits for every telephone line that is connected to a key set. As a result, the installation process is both expensive and time-consuming. In many cases, the labor and installation charges will account for as much as 25 to 30 percent of the cost of an electromechanical key system for a small business. A 1A2 system with eight or nine key sets will usually cost between $3,000 and $4,000.

The 1A2s represent less than 30 percent of the key systems in offices today. They have been replaced for the most part by electronic key systems, which outperform the 1A2's in feature and function because they are based on computer technology. While 1A2s can be configured to provide such options as intercom, office paging, music-on-hold, and speakerphone, the electronic systems offer these plus all sorts of additional features, including speed-dialing, last-number redial, call forwarding (in which you can route a call automatically to another phone in the same office if you're unavailable), and time and message displays, which allow you to see, on a liquid crystal display, messages, the time, and how long you've been on a call. (The last feature is great for lawyers and other professionals who bill by the clock.)

Instead of requiring twenty-five separate two-wire circuits for every incoming line, as 1A2's do, the new systems also have the advantage of using only three or four pairs of wires per phone. That makes the installation job cheaper, faster, and neater to the eye.

At the high end of the key market, there are even more elaborate electronic systems known as "hybrid keys," which offer users the kind of elaborate cost-control and productivity-enhancing features that previously were only available in much larger and more expensive computer-switching systems known as PBXs (for Private Branch Exchanges). These features include least-cost routing, in which the system automatically selects the cheapest long-distance carrier for the call you wish to make; call accounting, which uses computer software to provide you with a comprehensive record of where your staff is calling, how long they've been talking, and what long-distance carriers they are using in the process; and toll restriction, which enables you to fight employee call abuse by controlling which of your employees' phones can dial long-distance.

Electronic systems are generally 10 to 20 percent more expensive than 1A2s. Since the size limits for electronic systems are strictly defined, they also cannot be expanded the way the 1A2s can. Also because every manufacturer's electronic key system works differently, equipment from different manufacturers is usually incompatible with another. Despite these handicaps, you'll probably want to buy an electronic key system rather than a 1A2 today. Electronic keys are easier and cheaper to install, cost much less to move, and offer a lot more function for the price. They also look more stylish.

Mini-PBX's

Key systems, especially the hybrid ones, have become so sophisticated that it's hard to imagine a small business whose requirements couldn't be met with key technology. We would even go so far as to say that we see no real need for you to look beyond the key market in shopping for a small-business phone system. We would be remiss not to mention, however, that as hybrid key systems have developed PBX-like capabilities, there are now powerful mini-PBX's that may be suitable for businesses requiring just a few lines.

In a key system, each line comes in from the phone company on a separate circuit. The switching mechanism for selecting a line and obtaining a dial tone is in the phone on your desk. By punching one or another of the line buttons on your phone, a dial tone is immediately available to you from the telephone company's central office. In a PBX, by contrast, all the office phones are connected to one large central switch, which means that all traffic on the network must be routed through this switch. To get an outside line on a PBX, you have to ask the central switch for clearance by dialing "9."

One advantage of mini-PBXs over hybrid keys is in the kinds of phones required for their system. Unlike key systems, which require expensive multi-button phones to function effectively, PBXs are just as useful whether you use inexpensive single-line phones throughout your office or the more costly multi-button models.

PBXs are also more likely to communicate in digital code. (For an explanation of digital technology, see Chapter 23.) That could be important to you if you expect to be transmitting lots of data over the phone lines.

For most small businesses, key systems are still likely to be preferable to mini-PBXs. Not only are key systems generally cheaper, easier to use, and easier to install than PBXs, but in many places the local phone rates for PBX lines are twice as much as for key system lines. There's no good reason for this discrepancy in rates, but the discrepancy persists.

CHAPTER 21 Buying Smart

In shopping for a telephone system, the first question to ask is, "Do I need a new telephone system?" The answer, if you are just beginning your business, is easy. A business without a phone is no business at all. If you don't already own your phones and your company is moving to a new location, you have no choice but to arrange for new phones.

The tougher question is what to do if you already have phones, you aren't moving, and you have lots of other demands on your time. If you have phones that make hearing difficult, that break down frequently, or are so often busy that your customers can't get through, they are clearly costing you money. But if your phone bills seem low, your service is fine, and you're not anticipating any major changes in your business, you may think the answer is, "if the wagon ain't broke, don't fix it." So much has happened in the telephone world of late, however, that if you haven't looked carefully at your phone costs in the last two years, you could probably cut your phone bills by 20 to 40 percent. There will also be cases in which a review of your telephone system may lead you to upgrade your equipment in order to increase your overall office efficiency, even though that may raise your monthly telephone bill somewhat. A newer, more efficient telephone system may enable you to make major savings on time, personnel, mailing costs, and other administrative expenses. The question becomes not whether you can afford to change, but whether you can afford *not* to.

To make that decision, you'll need facts, facts that fit your business, not someone else's. The telephone vendors will help you, but only if you ask them the right questions. If you let them into your chicken coop without supervision, you might regret the outcome, extremely.

As with any other business in which confusion reigns, the telephone industry has spawned a whole species known as "telecommunications consultants," whose bill of goods is to analyze your telephone needs and advise you on what to do— for fees which are frequently substantial, of course. If you employ fewer than a dozen people, forget consultants. To do the job right, the consultant will have to learn how your business works. But you already know your business better than a consultant ever will. All the consultant will be doing is borrowing your watch to tell you what time it is. The truth is, profit margins for telephone consultants in the six-line market are so slim that it's extremely difficult for them to do a job well and still make any money.

Integrate Your Phone Decision and Your Overall Business Plan

Whether you're a restaurant owner or a dry cleaner, an orthopedic surgeon or a plumbing contractor, you should always keep in mind that a phone system is merely a means to an end, never an end in itself. It's crucial in choosing phones that you get a system that fits your overall business plan for the next five years. Telephone technology is changing so quickly that trying to plan beyond this point is ill-advised.

Of course, you don't know exactly what's ahead for your business over the next five years. But you should have at least a rough idea of what you hope and expect will happen to your business in that time-frame. At prices of $500 to $1000 per line for a new phone system, it would be foolish not to factor that into your phone decision. Suppose you're planning a major corporate acquisition next year. You wouldn't want to buy a phone system that couldn't be expanded to fit your new situation. Or suppose you have a watch repair business but are thinking about opening a travel agency. You wouldn't want to limit yourself to the plain black telephone that sufficed when the only calls you had to make were to check the time of day.

In the six-line market, which can mean systems with over a dozen extension phones, letting a salesperson load you up with features that you don't really need is usually a more serious problem than under-buying. But whether you base your purchasing decision on a conservative or optimistic growth projection, buy a system that can easily be expanded to allow for more telephone lines and calling functions, should you need them.

Buying vs. Leasing

You can't resolve the question of whether to buy or lease your phone system until you've thought about your outlook for the next five years. From a tax perspective, the laws are stacked in favor of buying. First, you are entitled to claim 10 percent of the system's purchase price as an investment tax credit. Second, you can depreciate the balance over five years. While leasing allows you to deduct your annual rental fees as an expense, the savings there aren't likely to match the tax benefits of buying. Besides, when you buy the equipment, it's yours.

Nevertheless, for businesses that are just opening, or ones whose outlook for the next few years is fraught with uncertainty, leasing can still make sense. Not only is there less front-end cost, but you don't get locked into a system that may prove incompatible with the way your business evolves. Unless you fall squarely into this category, however, buying your phone equipment is the economically practical thing to do.

Choosing Vendors

We're great believers in the free enterprise system. We think having choices and making decisions are the spice of life. But as we're the first to concede, the tremendous proliferation of vendors in the telephone business since the late 1960s makes your decision as to whom to buy from a potential nightmare. At last count there were over 3500 equipment vendors with visions of your money dancing in their heads. Twenty years ago, the only alternative was AT&T. In most metropolitan areas today, there will be at least a dozen excellent vendors that can serve your needs well. You'll want proposals from three or four, but that's enough. While getting a phone system in place is important, don't forget that it's not your main line of business, it's only a means to an end.

No matter what your business and your needs, start by contacting AT&T. It's not likely to be the cheapest and may not be the best for what you want, but it's still the standard by which all other equipment vendors must be judged. After all, the AT&T family invented the telephone, and its Bell Lab engineers and Western Electric factories have been turning out phones longer than anyone else in the world.

Choosing the other vendors on your list also need not bog you down. If you're short of names, ask your business friends if they can recommend a vendor, or look in the pages of *The Wall Street Journal*. With all the competition in the industry today, not a day goes by without the *Journal* carrying ads for several of the leading equipment makers. Another alternative is to buy the book, *Which Phone System Should I Buy?* by Harry Newton, available for $39.95 from Telecom Library (1-800-LIBRARY). Nor is there anything wrong with looking in the Yellow Pages under "Telephone Equipment and Systems" and picking out a few familiar names. In some cases you will remember companies because of their ads. In other cases it will be because of their reputation in other consumer electronics fields.

While we can't recommend specific companies that are best for you, the following equipment makers or distributors are well-known for their small-business systems products: AT&T, Comdial, Crest, Executone, GTE, Hitachi, Inter-Tel, ITT, Iwatsu, Mitel, NEC, Northern Telecom, San/Bar, Stromberg-Carlson, TIE/Communications, Toshiba, Walker Telecommunications, and Webcor. Both Sears Roebuck & Company and Radio Shack are also making a point of marketing telephone systems to the small-business community.

Preparing for the Vendor Visit

A good phone system is one that fits your company's needs, and a good salesperson's proposal ought to reflect those needs. But even the best vendors must rely on you to explain how your business works. To do that well, before ever meeting a salesperson, you need to spend a couple of hours analyzing what phones mean to your business.

If you're just starting a business and don't have phones yet, ask yourself, "How will my business use the phone?" Real estate agents and stockbrokers will be on the phone all the time; doctors will need answering services. Lawyers make frequent calls to associates within their firms; grocers may rarely need the phone at all. Always have your five-year plan firmly in mind so that you can factor into your analysis how your business is likely to change.

Where your business is already open and your telephone habits are established, you should ask whether your current phone system is serving your business well. Start by drawing up a list of all the phones your company has and where they're located. Take note of who uses them and how. Are some of your employees swamped with calls? Do you miss messages when the staff takes off for lunch? Might there be a need for speaker phones, an office paging system, or conference calling? How much time and money could be saved with touch-tone dialing? Your staff will know what the problems are. Be sure to ask them.

Finally, collect several months of phone bills to show the salesperson. That way both you and he will know exactly what your telephone costs are now, and what you'd expect to beat if you were to make a change. While you have the bills out, see if there have been any significant changes in your telephone charges lately. Any big increases may be a red flag showing that it's time for you to change your ways.

Meeting with the Vendor

You've called three sales reps; the first has arrived. From the moment he or she walks through your door, ask yourself, is this someone who is interested in my business and my needs, or is this a hit-and-run operator whose only concern is to turn a fast buck and get out of Dodge before any problems develop? When you're buying a phone system, the kind of hardware you choose and the price you pay may turn out to be far less important in the end than the quality of your vendor's commitment to keep you happy. While we don't expect you to apply the same standards in picking a telephone vendor as you would in selecting a spouse, you need to ask yourself, is the vendor represented by this salesperson some-one I'd like dealing with over the long term?

Buy Functions, Not Features

Maseratis are great, but if what you really need is a station wagon to drive your three kids to school in the snow, then it would be foolish to buy the sports car. The same is true for phone systems. As dazzling as many of the small-business phone systems are today, it would be ridiculous for you to buy lots of bells and whistles that have no practical value to your business.

Good salespersons will know this without having to be re-minded. They'll always try to emphasize for you the benefits a particular feature might have for your business, rather than to describe various features in the abstract. Don't waste your time on vendors who dwell on features but can't talk to you about benefits.

At the same time, never forget that a sales rep's job is to sell, and that even the most honorable among them is there to sell you something. As you listen to their pitches, keep in mind that like their counterparts in the auto business, they have higher profit margins when they sell the equivalent of power windows and quadraphonic tape decks than for stripped-down compacts. If your vendor can't easily explain the benefits of a special feature, you don't need it.

Warranties and Service

In most small businesses, it's a disaster if the phone system crashes. That's why strong warranties and top-quality service and maintenance are crucial. A good warranty insures that the vendor, not you, will bear the legal and financial responsibility of fixing or replacing your new phone system within the warranty period if it doesn't work. That's important protection against buying a lemon. In most cases the manufacturer's warranty on telephone equipment is one year, but at least two independent phone makers, Northern Telcom and Comdial, are offering two-year warranties.

The key maintenance and service question is, how fast can you fix phones? To help you make that determination, you should ask the salesperson if the vendor repairs your equipment or farms the work out. Is the repair work done on-site, or is the faulty equipment shipped back to a central facility? Where is it? Will the company respond to emergencies twenty-four hours a day? What are the rates for maintenance and service?

As the proprietor of a small business, you have lots of things to worry about without having to deal with a phone system that's gone kaput. Should that misfortune befall you, you won't want to hear excuses, you'll want to be able to get a repair team out to your site with a snap of your fingers. Choose a vendor who can make repairs. It might be worth paying as much as 10 to 15 percent more than the low bidder would require for that comfort factor.

A Word on Wiring

While we've cautioned you not to waste money on capacity or features that you don't really need, you should know that it's much easier to add new phones, switches, and features to your system as your business grows than it is to bring new wiring into your office or run it through your walls. When it comes to wiring, err on the side of ordering too much wire from the street to your place of business. When you're planning your interior space, don't skimp on wiring the walls for extra telephone outlets. You never know when you'll have to rearrange the furniture and move your employees around.

For You, the "Office of the Future" Is Still the Future

One of the great buzzwords of the Information Age is the "office of the future." That's the notion that your office telephones and computers should all link up in a dazzling array of voice and data communications capabilities that will produce magical improvements in productivity and profitability. It's a concept that journalists and other seers love to write about, and that office automation salesmen want to browbeat you into believing. Forget it. For your size operation, the "office of the future" doesn't exist yet. If the IBMs and the Exxons of the world haven't figured out how to "network" their offices fully yet, there's no reason why you ought to feel you should.

Don't confuse the decision to buy a telephone system with the decision to buy a personal computer. Personal computers can be a great asset for a small business, but at this point they are still an issue separate and distinct from buying a phone system. If you try to combine the two decisions, you'll get so hopelessly confused that you'll never accomplish anything. For now, select your phone system with your voice communications needs in mind, and use a modem on your computer (see Chapter 17) to manage your data communications requirements.

Financing Your Acquisition

The typical small business phone system of six lines or so will cost $3,000 to $4,000. It will almost never make sense for you to pay cash on the barrelhead for an investment of this size and type. Financing a phone deal is not very different from financing a car. In its eagerness to close a sale with you, your vendor will generally be delighted to help you arrange financing. The question is, at what price.

In almost every case, your vendor can steer you to a bank with which it has close relations in order to arrange a loan. You also have the option of going to your own bank or to another financial institution in your community. Many vendors will also lease you a system. In addition, they will know of independent leasing firms that will buy the equipment you have selected and then lease it back to you on a long-term basis.

To calculate the cost of a phone system, always bear in mind the tax implications. Under the current law, by purchasing, you qualify to claim both a 10-percent investment tax credit on the sticker price, and to depreciate the equipment over a useful life of five years. By leasing, you gain the right to write off your yearly leasing charges as an ordinary cost of doing business. But you will not be entitled to claim the investment tax credit or deduct the interest charges on the loan. Remember that the difference between a $5,000 and $6,000 system is substantially less than $1,000 when you figure in the tax angle. (U.S. Treasury Department proposals for a radical revision of the tax code could affect the tax benefits for purchasing your own telephone system, but passage of such legislation is highly uncertain at this time.)

A Few Other Words of Advice

- Be sure you know all the installation charges before you sign.
- Be sure all sales taxes are included in the purchase price.
- Be sure you know how long your vendor's service guarantee runs, and what the cost of a service contract or work by the hour will be when the initial guarantee expires.
- Be sure you know what it will cost you to cancel the job before completion.
- Be sure that your payment schedule allows you to withhold final payment until installation is completed to your satisfaction.
- Be sure that the system you're getting is the one you're paying for. Some vendors will charge you for new phones, but provide you with refurbished equipment.

Installation of Your System

Not all vendors do their own installations. Be skeptical of those that don't. It's much better to have the vendor that sold you the system install it, so that you can hold the vendor directly responsible for doing the job right.

Expect that the actual installation process, or "cutover" as it is called in the business, will take at least a full day, or night. Doing the job on a weekend or at night is preferable if it can be arranged, because it's less disruptive to your business. In any case, don't do what a news organization that we know, and love all too well, did recently. On the day of a critical editing deadline, it arranged for the offices to be rewired for a new phone system while its editors were trying to work.

Where the installation of your system requires new wiring from the outside to your place of business by the local phone company, allow plenty of time for the phone company to do its part. Then, to be on the safe side, add another couple of weeks' leeway to the schedule.

Before you accept your vendor's cutover, you should have the vendor's representative give you a "walk-through" of the system so that you can check whether everything that was ordered was installed in proper working order. This walk-through is sometimes called the final acceptance test. Don't write any more checks to the vendor unless you're satisfied with the walk-through.

Training to Use the System Effectively

The greatest system in the world won't be of any value to you unless you know how to use it. It's your vendor's responsibility to provide the training. It's your responsibility to take the training seriously. Don't send a temporary secretary to represent the company in the vendor's training course. Send your best. Expect that the process will take at least a day.

To make sure the training sticks, arrange for the vendor to have someone on your premises a second day to answer questions and provide whatever additional help your staff might need. Go the extra mile to insure that your investment pays off.

How Long Will It All Take?

It sounds like a big job, and it is. We estimate that in most small business cases it takes between six to ten weeks to decide on a telephone system and negotiate the contract. During that time you and your co-workers are likely to have to spend between twelve and fifteen hours focusing on the problem. If you add another day for the cutover, and a day and a half for training, the total time required is about a week. While it would be nice to spend that time on something else, the question is, can you afford not to deal with your own telephone survival yourself?

CHAPTER **22** Small
Business
Service
Options

We've devoted a lot of space to buying systems because equipment charges are something over which you have some control. Unfortunately, that's much less true when it comes to your options on local service. As we discussed in Chapter 8, the reorganization of the telephone industry is producing a rapid climb in local rates for both residential and business customers. But unlike the long-distance field, where you have a host of carriers to choose from if you don't like AT&T's prices, local service is still a monopoly of the local phone company. That leaves you with little choice but to swallow any local rate increases that your local phone company may win from your state regulatory authorities.

In the residential market, where subscribers still have a choice between flat-rate and measured-service plans in most states, heavy local callers can control their costs somewhat by electing flat-rate service. While flat rates are going up on a percentage basis as least as much, and in most cases more, than measured rates, flat-rate service enables residential users to set a ceiling on their local monthly charges without having to restrict their local calling.

To business customers with heavy local calling needs, flat-rate service is also a very attractive option. Unfortunately, it's a choice that might not be open to you. In many states today, the only option that the local telephone company is making available to businesses is measured service. That means that you pay as you go. It also means that if your employees like to gab on the phone, it's your nickel. And dimes. And dollars. If the gabbing is long-distance, the problem is that much worse.

There are ways to keep unnecessary calling, and thus unnecessary bills, under control. Most modern key systems can be equipped with a feature known as Call-Detail Recording (Station Message-Detail Recording is another name), which gives you a record of each local and long-distance call made on your company phones and how long it lasted. This should make it easy for you to identify habitual abusers. A cheaper but effective alternative is to watch closely for a day how the phones in your office are being used, and then let your staff know if you have problems. In a small business, that shouldn't be hard. While we're not proposing that you come on like the KGB, your employees should understand that when they make personal calls, you're paying.

Centrex

In addition to its "plain vanilla" local service, the local telephone company offers an enhanced service known in different states as Centrex, Centron, ESSX, or Centraflex. By subscribing to Centrex, which is the service's most frequently used name, businesses receive from their local telephone company a package of special features similar to those on an electronic key system or PBX on their premises. The features include speed-dialing, call-hold, call conferencing with two separately located outside parties, and telephone-to-telephone intercom within the office.

To provide these special features, the local telephone company simply programs a piece of its huge central office switch to provide your lines with these added capabilities. The effects are the same as if it were your own key system or PBX controlling the circuits, but instead of having a small switch of your own to direct the traffic, you're sharing the use of a much larger switch. From an engineering perspective, it makes no difference whatsoever whether the traffic instructions are coming from your end or the phone company's end of the line.

Until recently, Centrex's price structure made it economically unviable for very small businesses. But with the breakup of the Bell System and the local telephone companies' worry about losing much of their large business customers' traffic to "bypass" (see page 91), almost all the former Bell operating companies have revised their Centrex rate structures to attract businesses of as few as half a dozen phones. In some states, you can now get basic Centrex service for as low as $10 a month per line. For a few extra dollars a month, you can often get such features as call-detail recording and least-cost routing, which is an invaluable tool in cutting long-distance bills. (For more on least-cost routing, see page 223.)

Before you invest a lot of money in your own office switch, make a point of examining Centrex. While there's no investment tax credit or accelerated depreciation if you lease rather than purchase, Centrex has become, in some cases, an excellent alternative to buying. First, you don't have the kind of initial capital costs associated with buying, rather than leasing, your switching capability. Second, you don't have the heavy installation charges that come with owning your own switch. Third, it's usually both easy and cheap to expand your Centrex service if you guess wrong about your company's growth. Fourth, you save space in your office by having your switch located at the telephone company. Fifth, if any switching problems develop, it will be the responsibility of the local telephone company to have them fixed, not you.

Because for many small businesses, Centrex is now a viable alternative to buying a small electronic key system, a natural competition has developed between companies selling key systems and the telephone companies leasing Centrex. As the customer, you may be able to turn this rivalry to your advantage. While state regulatory authorities generally don't allow local telephone companies to compete with equipment vendors by cutting Centrex

prices below the rates filed with the state, this is gradually beginning to change. If you live in a state where the local telephone
company has been given the flexibility to compete with equipment
vendors on price, make the equipment vendor better the price
quoted by your Centrex salesperson, and vice versa.

Long-Distance Options

If you have a pizza parlor or a dentist's office, you're not likely
to worry much about long-distance service in your business. But if
you have long-distance bills of $20 a month or more, you're a
candidate for one of the alternative long-distance companies that
have taken the field in competition with AT&T. If you're a very
heavy long-distance caller, or if you call one geographic area or one
specific number very frequently, you may benefit from using one of
several specialized private service offerings available from AT&T
and a few of its competitors. We'll take up some of these private
service options in a moment, but first there's the question of
subscribing to one of the alternative long-distance services to
AT&T.

Assuming that your business is at least a moderate long-distance
user, you almost certainly could save some money by using one of
the alternative long-distance services. Since start-up fees and all
but the most modest minimum monthly charges have been eliminated by all the major long-distance competitors of AT&T, there's
almost no reason not to sign up with one or more of the alternative
carriers.

As a small business, the impact of equal access and the analysis
you must do to choose a carrier won't really differ from that of the
average residential customer. In both cases, the issues are twofold:
what are the rates and what is the quality? We suggest you look
back to Chapter 10 for our advice on how to approach the matter.
We would add only one point here. Several of the leading carriers,
Allnet, GTE Sprint, ITT, and MCI among them, offer sizable
volume discounts to heavy callers. These discounts can bring your

bill down considerably. Keep in mind that because of all the competition in the long-distance market, carriers are constantly revamping their rate structures. You should review your long-distance options periodically to determine which plan is best for you.

AT&T PRO America

This discount plan can apply to any AT&T customer, but it is designed for small businesses. For a $25 monthly fee, AT&T gives a 15 percent discount on direct-dialed interstate long-distance calls, day or night. The service, AT&T claims, ought to be attractive to about a million of its current customers who use daytime long-distance between six and fifty hours a month; a business that makes more than fifty hours of calls a month could probably save more money using WATS (see below). One advantage of AT&T PRO America over WATS is that the customer gets a detailed monthly statement listing all calls made during that period. If you think a plan like AT&T PRO America could save you money, you should also check the offerings of the alternative long-distance carriers; some of them may have even better deals.

AT&T Opportunity Calling for Business

This is a marketing gimmick that AT&T bills as a "special program designed for small businesses," and that we include because you've probably seen it advertised heavily. For every dollar your business spends on AT&T long-distance service, you earn a dollar's credit toward the purchase of a variety of products and services listed in a catalogue published by AT&T. The offerings include computers, typewriters, photocopiers, and courier services. You must spend $15 a month to qualify, and can earn a maximum of $300 a month in credits. If you're the type that buys the portable television offered to you by American Express, or the briefcase peddled by Citibank Visa, then Opportunity Calling may be for you. You'll have to judge this for yourself.

Wide Area Telecommunications Service (WATS)

Wide Area Telecommunications Service, or WATS as it is known, is a special AT&T phone line that provides interstate long-distance service to high-volume callers at great potential savings. Next to basic dial-tone and dial-up long-distance service, AT&T WATS is probably the best known but least understood service that the telephone industry provides. A WATS line is not, as many people believe, a way of getting unlimited long-distance calling for a flat monthly rate. Besides hefty installation fees and a fixed monthly access fee, WATS customers are also charged for individual calls based on where you call, how long you talk, and the time of day and day of the week you phone. The fact that the meter is running on every call is often overlooked because most WATS bills don't provide a breakout of individual calls; they only report total calling minutes for the month and total charges for that calling.

Depending on where you call and how long you're on the phone, AT&T WATS could be an excellent deal for you, however. That's because of the way WATS tallies mileage charges and discounts for volume calling. Under the WATS plan, subscribers must specify how big a calling radius their businesses require. In doing so, they may choose from among six broad service bands, with Band One entitling them to use WATS to call a few neighboring states, Band Two extending this radius by a few more states, and so on, until the entire continental United States, plus Hawaii, Puerto Rico, and the U.S. Virgin Islands, are made available in Band Five, and Alaska is added in Band Six. The higher the band, the higher the monthly usage charge.

There are several factors that work to offset these charges, however. For example, the usage charges for calling on WATS are substantially lower than they would be for dialing the same numbers over ordinary long-distance. There are also very generous volume discounts for heavy WATS callers. Assuming your calls each month average at least a minute, WATS also has the advantage of billing calls to the nearest second, while AT&T's ordinary long-distance service rounds your calls up to the nearest full minute.

To have a WATS line installed, you must pay a $51.80 "service ordering charge" plus a connection charge of $123 per line. There is also a $31.65 monthly service fee per line. Because the installation charges and monthly service fees for WATS are substantially higher than for ordinary long-distance service, you have to be a fairly heavy long-distance user for WATS to make sense. But if your staff is running monthly long-distance bills of over $300, you may benefit from WATS.

Toll-Free 800 Numbers

AT&T 800 Service is a plan that allows customers to call your company over a toll-free number that begins with 800, and have their calls billed to your account at volume discount rates. It is similar to AT&T WATS except that it applies to incoming, rather than outgoing, long distance traffic. For many companies, AT&T's toll-free 800 Service is just what is needed to motivate a customer's purchase. By allowing customers to call you long-distance at your expense, you make it easy for shop-at-home buyers to place their orders. To many businesses, an 800 number is equally as important for handling customer questions on service, billing, and other problems.

The geographical coverage and pricing for AT&T 800 Service are based on the same six geographic bands that are used for AT&T WATS. The higher the band you subscribe to, the wider the area from which you can be called toll-free. Marketing specialists claim that by including a toll-free number with your ads, you can improve your sales by as much as 20 to 50 percent.

In subscribing to 800 Service, you can pick a number that spells your company's name or is otherwise a reminder of your business, if it is available. Neiman-Marcus uses 800-NEIMANS, for instance. TWA's number is 800-AIRLINE.

800 Service is available on an intrastate as well as interstate basis, but the rates are different in each case.

Specially Dedicated Private Lines

While WATS can be a help to companies with heavy long-distance calling requirements over a broad geographical range, there are two other types of private lines that may be of more value to you if your calling destinations are more pinpointed. One is known as a foreign exchange, or FX line. It is for businesses that need to call a single distant city with great regularity. With FX service, you get a private line that links your office with the local central switch in the city you need to call. The dial tone you hear when you pick up your FX line is coming from the local switch in your city of destination. To complete the call, all you have to do is dial your party's local number, as if you were calling from down the street rather than from out-of-state. If there are parties on the other end who know the number of your FX line, they can also reach you with just a local call on that line.

Since FX lines are billed on a flat monthly rate, it costs you no more for an individual call than it would if you were making that call locally in your destination city. Our office in Washington, D.C., has an FX line to New York so that we can call both our editors and our sources in the New York business world cheaply and easily. For the right parties, FX lines can be one of the last great deals left in the business, but they're not for everyone so be careful. Most FX lines come from AT&T, but several of the alternative long-distance carriers offer them on certain routes, as well.

The second private-line alternative is the tie-line, which connects you with a single out-of-town phone, rather than with a distant city. Many companies use tie-lines to link themselves to a branch office or factory. Your tie-line can be programmed so that the other phone will ring as soon as one phone is picked up. You don't even have to dial. Tie-lines are available from both AT&T and most of the alternative long-distance carriers.

Least-Cost Routing

Although we have mentioned least-cost routing a couple of times already, we'd like to add just a little more about it here. Your telephone switch or the local phone company's central office can be programmed to route your long-distance calls to the least expensive long-distance carrier available to you. It puts the onus on the machine, and not the caller, to sort through the alternative routes and prices and make a quick and economical decision about how to complete the call. With the proliferation of hundreds of long-distance companies, offering hundreds of variations in rates, Least-Cost Routing is a service well worth installing for any company with substantial long-distance costs. It is becoming a standard feature of most modern key systems and mini-PBXs, and is also available at a modest cost on Centrex, if you prefer not to buy your own switch.

Shared-Tenant Services

This is an idea whose time is coming. In a few areas of the country, notably Texas, New York, and Washington, D.C., developers and landlords are beginning to install sophisticated telephone switches in their buildings to offer a whole range of enhanced communications services to their tenants and clients. Instead of having individual offices lease or buy their own switching capacity, the idea is to have all the tenants share a large PBX switch somewhere in the building, in much the same way that the local telephone company uses its central office switch to provide Centrex.

Don't think that this trend to "smart buildings" is mainly of interest to large businesses with very extensive telecommunications and computing needs. In fact, it may be that this option is best suited to small businesses, which appreciate the advantages of state-of-the-art communications, but don't have the time, the money, or the expertise to develop their own system. Among the services these "smart buildings" are capable of providing on a shared-tenant basis are teleconferencing, message forwarding, electronic mail, and low-cost long-distance telephone connections. Several leading developers, including the huge Canadian firm, Olympia & York, and the Dallas company, Lincoln Property, now plan to build such capabilities into all their major office projects. A number of shopping center developers are even planning to offer shared-communications services to their small retail tenants.

There will be risks in casting your lot with such facilities. One large risk is that if the developer, landlord, or management agent charged with operating your building's "smarts" turns out to be inept, unlucky, or both, the system on which you're depending for your communications goes down. These are, after all, the same people who sometimes screw up the heat and air-conditioning. But the fact that there's so much innovative thinking taking place about telecommunications may be the most promising sign yet that the breakup of Ma Bell eventually will turn out for the best.

23 FuturePhone: An Array of Wonders

Going to Los Angeles tomorrow? You'll never be out of touch. Your personal phone number will ring at Aunt Nettie's house, where you'll be staying.

Do you wonder who could be calling at this hour? Just glance at your phone. The number calling you is displayed on a little screen.

Are you at home alone, when you'd really like to play a game of bridge? Dial up a game with others who are also at home. You can talk to the other players and see your hand and the dummy's on a video screen.

These are telephone fantasies today. But they will be realities by the end of this decade. For the telephone system, top-to-bottom, is undergoing extremely rapid, far-reaching change that will substitute an array of wonders for Plain Old Telephone Service. "Ten years ago we talked about cost and performance," says Warren E. Falconer, director of AT&T Bell Laboratories' transmission network and services planning center. They're still important, he says, but now "we talk about new services. It is the new services that are fun." And when we talk about new communications services, says Casimir Skrzypczak, vice-president for network planning at Bell Communications Research, which performs research and engineering for the local Bell operating companies, "you are really limited only by your imagination."

New services is just another way of saying that how we communicate, how we seek information, how we deal with others will change substantially. The changes will come because of fast-moving telephone technology. Will you be dehumanized in the process? Not likely. Communication is one of the most human of all activities. The new technologies ought to bring you closer to your fellows—closer at least to those whose calls you choose to answer.

See Who Is Calling You

Today when you dial a number, your call is completed to the telephone you are trying to reach. The number of the telephone from which you called is sent only to a billing computer. That is so you are charged properly. Under a new scheme being tested in Harrisburg, Pennsylvania, and Orlando, Florida, the calling number is sent all the way through the network to the telephone at the other end. With this "custom local area signaling services," or CLASS, you can see the number of the person who is calling you displayed on your phone.

CLASS can change your relationship with those who call. Now, when the phone rings, you have no idea who is calling you. You'd better answer, you say; it might be important. On the other hand, it could be someone you don't want to talk to at all. You have no way of knowing. So you answer the phone, and it's a fast-talking salesman who wants you to try out a new long-distance service. If you could see the number that is calling, you could decide on the spot whether to answer or not.

That's just the beginning. You will be able to block certain numbers permanently. If you don't ever want to hear from someone, you'll be able to tell the telephone company, and calls from that number will never be sent to you again. When someone tries to call you from that blocked phone, he'll get a recording explaining that his calls will not be accepted. You may be able to do the recording, yourself. That way you could send an insulting rejection to someone automatically, at any time of day or night. Of course, your protection is not complete. He can always go to another phone and dial.

You will be able to tell the phone company that calls from certain parties, such as your spouse, your boss, or your mother-in-law, deserve special attention. If you have Call Waiting, for example, and you are talking to someone when the boss tries to call, you'll hear a distinctive tone that means one of your special people is trying to reach you. If you have Call Forwarding, so that calls are sent to another number when no one answers your phone, you can arrange that only certain numbers are forwarded. After all, who wants to have a call forwarded from an aggressive long-distance salesman?

If the phone you have just called is busy, you will be able to instruct your phone to continue dialing for the next thirty minutes. When the party at the other end picks up, your phone will ring. If you think you missed an important call while you were away, you can simply tell your phone to call the last number that tried to call you. Surprise! It was the long-distance-service salesman who tried to call. Perhaps you need an answering machine. (See Chapter 13.) CLASS will make possible a whole new spectrum of technically advanced telephone answering machines. You will be able to have your answering machine select outgoing messages that are appropriate to the number of the call coming in. If the boss calls, for example, you can have your machine tell him or her that you are out working and won't be available for several hours. But if a member of your poker group calls, you can have your machine tell him or her where you are playing.

At first blush, CLASS appears to have certain Big Brother aspects. If your number is sent to the other end, you lose a certain anonymity. But the advantages will surely outweigh the disadvantages. These new services have the potential to make your telephone a better and safer friend. If you are so unfortunate as to receive an obscene or threatening phone call, you can see the caller's number and immediately notify the phone company or the police. CLASS could help improve computer security, too. If a computer "hacker" illegally tries to break into a computer by using the telephone, the hacker's number would be recorded by the computer. That would be a strong deterrent to illegal hacking.

Digital Wonders

New telephone services are becoming possible because telephone technology is changing so rapidly. The way information is moved through the entire telephone system is being transformed from analog to digital. Oh, you say, that's nice, but what does it really mean? It means the telephone system is making an enormous leap in power, similar to what happened in transportation with the change from sail to steam in ships, or from horsedrawn buggies to automobiles. The importance of this digital leap is almost impossible to overstate. It is almost impossible to explain, too, but we're going to try. For if you grasp the outlines of the technical changes, you can see the wonders that are coming.

The telephone system was designed from the beginning to convert sound waves from your voice into electric waves that are sent along wires. At the other end, the electric waves are converted back to sound waves. Since the electric waves are a continuous representation of the sound waves—they are analogous to the sound waves, in other words—this type of transmission is called analog transmission.

The advent of computers brought a new way of handling information. A computer "thinks" by turning little switches "on" or "off." These "on" and "off" switches inside silicon chips are represented mathematically by the numbers zero and one—as *b*inary dig*its,* in other words, or *bits.* Computers talk to each other by transmitting bits over a wire as electric pulses. In order for computers to communicate over analog phone lines, in fact, it is necessary to convert the computer's digital signals into analog for transmission (that's what a modem does), then back to digital at the other end.

Telephone companies are big users of digital computers. All the huge new telephone switches, the machines that route your call to the correct destination, are actually big computers. In fact, your analog voice call is converted to digital so it can run through a big switch. Then it is often converted back to analog for transmission the rest of the way.

Digital transmission of data is far cheaper and faster than analog, it allows computers to be linked directly, and, by their nature, digital signals suffer much less distortion than analog. As a result, the whole information world is going digital. Demand for transmission of digital data is skyrocketing, growing far faster than any telephone forecaster dreamed would be possible. All our computers, including the proliferating personal computers (which the forecasters didn't see coming), speak digital. The new internal telephone systems used by businesses are nearly all digital. It is even cheaper to transmit naturally analog signals, like voice and video, as digital information.

Sound waves from our voices are converted to electric waves as before, then the curves of the electric waves are measured thousands of times a second and the dimensions of the curves are sent over a network as streams of binary numbers. At the receiving end, the numbers are used to reconstruct the electric waves so they can be used to make sound waves again. Along the way, the binary numbers representing the sound of your voice look just like the binary numbers representing a corporation's payroll moving from one computer to another or the binary numbers representing the video for the *CBS Evening News*. All that information is represented the same way, as a kind of "digital Esperanto."

Digital signals are clean and free of distortion because the pulses represent numbers. At each amplification point on the network, the same numbers, sharp as the originals, are sent on their way. By contrast, any electrical disturbance on an analog signal changes the shape of the electrical waves, so the disturbance is amplified along with the rest of the signal. You often hear the disturbance as static.

The best and cheapest way to transmit digital information is on "lightwave" or fiber-optic systems. Digital bits are sent over a thin glass strand as pulses of laser-generated light. The quicker the lasers pulse, the faster the data moves. The newest lightwave cables being laid by AT&T, for example, transmit data at a mind-numbing 1.7 gigabits per second. That's 1.7 billion bits of information a second, enough to carry 169,344 simultaneous telephone conversations—all on a piece of glass that looks like a piece of very thin fishing line. Put another way, that glass strand could send the entire contents of the Encyclopedia Britannica in less than two seconds.

Because the lightwave systems offer such high quality and are so cheap compared to other ways of moving data, companies are plowing an incredible amount of new fiber-optic cables into the ground. AT&T plans to open up 10,000 miles of new glass cables, as well as convert 9000 miles of microwave and 4500 miles of coaxial cables to digital transmission, between 1983 and the end of 1988. MCI and GTE Sprint say they will add 22,000 miles of fiber-optic cables, and several other companies are projecting big new networks. Railroads are even getting into the game. Two of them plan to build an 8,100-mile fiber-optic system on railroad rights-of-way by 1987. Indeed, if these companies build every new digital transmission line they say they are going to build, America's long-distance network will grow sixfold between 1985 and 1990. While it's likely not everything planned will be built, the growth in low-cost, high-speed data-transport capacity is simply stupendous.

What is going to be done with all that capacity? There are skeptics who believe it won't all be used, but they're like the people in the late 1940s who said that a handful of large computers could supply all the computational needs of the United States. As we all hook our personal computers onto the telephone network, as we hold more videoconferences, as we automate our factories, the need for data transport will grow and grow and grow. Judge Harold H. Greene, who presided over the AT&T divestiture trial, said recently, "Information will be to this period what steel and coal were fifty years ago." While this is doubtless true, there is an important difference between information and natural resources. After you mine coal for many years, the seams run out and the coal is gone. But our ability to produce and transmit information seems almost infinite.

The "Smart" Network

A digital telephone network that is controlled by digital computers "is getting a heck of a lot smarter than it was before," says
Skrzypczak. In the past, he explains, the telephone network was
pretty "dumb." Its intelligence was limited to deciding what to do
with the seven or ten digits you dialed and where to route your call.
But with telephone networks controlled by very large computers
that are connected by digital transmission links, it is possible for
the network to handle each call in a different way.

The telephone companies can, for example, maintain individual
records on each customer's needs and desires. When that customer makes a call—or someone calls that customer—the network
can pause for the briefest moment, send a message to its computer
database, ask if that customer wants special treatment, and respond as necessary. If you call an 800 number, for example, the
phone company's data base could direct that you should be
asked—by computer-generated synthetic speech—what you want.
If you wish to order something, you may be asked to tap a certain
key on your phone. If you want to complain, on the other hand,
you could be told to hit another key.

Greater computing capacity, or intelligence, in the telephone
system will make personal phone numbers possible. Instead of
having a number on your phone at home and another number on
your phone at work, you could have just one number. Whenever
you go to a new location, you simply advise the telephone system's
data base as to where you'll be, and your number will follow you
there. You will be able to tell the phone company what your
schedule will be, weeks ahead, if you know it.

Local telephone companies are gearing up to offer special data
services to business and residential users. Today, if your personal
computer, word processor, and security system use the telephone,
they tie up a phone line. It is possible, however, to send such low-
speed data over the same phone line as voice—and at the same

time. A lawyer might use his phone to talk to a client while at the same time—and using the same telephone line—his law clerk in the next room could use a terminal to call a remote information base to research a legal case.

Telephone companies say such a data service would cost much less than using a separate phone line for small computers. Better yet, the hourly rate would be substantially below that charged by present low-speed data networks. One regional telephone company claims it could transmit data for $1 an hour, compared to $6 or more for the data networks. But the company still hasn't persuaded the Federal Communications Commission to let it provide the new service. The company argues persuasively that the new data network "will make it possible for home and business customers to access information in countless data bases. It should make activities like home banking and shopping, videotex, electronic mail, bookkeeping and updating remote data bases widespread because they will be available—and affordable—to the average residential and business customer."

Today, voice and data move over many different kinds of networks. The growth in digital transmission will make it possible to replace them all with what engineers call Integrated Services Digital Networks, or ISDNs. That is a digital circuit to which any kind of digital machine can be connected, with a standard interface. All kinds of information can be carried on an ISDN simultaneously, from readings of a household water meter, to videotex, high-fidelity music, digital voice, and video. All this stuff would flow as immense streams of numbers. Some telephone companies will start testing ISDNs in 1986. They are expected to be available more widely by 1988.

Under an ISDN architecture, an individual customer such as a business, telephone experts say, could buy such a digital pipe and configure it on its own. Part of the capacity could be used to transport voice, part could be used to connect computers. Best of all, it could be changed rapidly, as needed. During the day, when everyone is sitting in his or her office, the bulk of the capacity could be split up and used for voice channels. At night, the same digital pipe could be used to transport huge volumes of data between computers. "It's very much like a water pipe that you size for the amount of water you expect to use at any point in time," explains Skrzypczak. "Sometimes you might be using that pipe to fill a swimming pool, sometimes to run a bunch of water fountains."

The New World

The new digital services are being eagerly devoured by large corporations, but they hold promise for the small businessperson, too. "In the new world, the digital world, people will be able to subscribe to a pool of services," says Bell Labs' Falconer. A small businessperson could have access to computerized information bases, data processing, teleconferencing, as well as videoconferencing and telephony services. The small businessperson today would have to order each service individually and pay for it all the time—at a price he can't afford. But he could afford to share the services with others. "What I think will happen is that the small businessman will pay a modest amount to sign up for this ability, then pay on a usage-basis instead of for dedicated lines," Falconer says.

Many telephone customers will be able to get digital service on their existing telephone lines, something available now only on expensive dedicated lines. If properly modified, ordinary copper-wire telephone circuits can, under ISDN, transmit and receive voice or digital data on two separate channels, and data on a third packet-switched channel—all at the same time. That one pair of wires can carry a total of 144 kilobits per second on three channels simultaneously, fifteen times more digital data than today's regular phone line can handle.

With so much new digital capacity coming on line and heavy competition in the long-distance data transportation business, there is strong pressure to offer new services. Some of these services will be strictly for fun. Falconer says, "I can envision that if I can't sleep at night I come down to my telephone and my screen and say, 'I want to play bridge.' I go to my data base and get coupled in with others who want to play." He says this will be feasible because the digital bits are getting cheaper every day, and you don't need as many of them.

There may even be another attempt at marketing a telephone that sends video pictures along with voice. That is because bits are getting cheap enough to make video feasible, at least for some business uses. Broadcast television requires a lot of bits. But it is possible to send lower-quality video with less than 1 percent as many bits as broadcast video requires.

Not everything new, however, is necessarily high-tech. Telephone companies are trying out a new service in which you dial a number and join in a free-for-all conversation with many others on the line. You can meet new friends, get into arguments, or simply listen to others gossip. Telephone people say the experimental "voice teleconferencing" service has proved to be very popular in tests. But then, it always was. In the early years of telephony, it was called a "party line."

Appendix
State Regulatory Commissions

Alabama
Alabama Public Service Commission
P.O. Box 991
Montgomery, AL 36130
205-832-3421

Alaska
Alaska Public Utilities Commission
420 L Street
Suite 100
Anchorage, AK 99501
907-276-6222

Arizona
Arizona Corporation Commission
1200 West Washington Street
Phoenix, AZ 85007
602-255-3931

Arkansas
Arkansas Public Service Commission
400 Union Station
Makham & Victory Streets
Little Rock, AR 72201
501-371-1794

California
Public Utilities Commission
350 McAllister Street
San Francisco, CA 94102
415-557-1487

Colorado
Colorado Public Utilities Commission
Logan Tower, Office Level 2
1580 Logan Street
Denver, CO 80203
303-866-3156

Connecticut
Connecticut Public Utilities Commission
1 Central Park Plaza
New Britain, CT 06051
203-827-1553

Delaware
Delaware Public Service Commission
1560 South DuPont Highway
Dover, DE 19901
302-736-4247

District of Columbia
Public Service Commission of the District of Columbia
451 Indiana Avenue NW
Washington, DC 20001
202-727-3050

Florida
Florida Public Service Commission
101 East Gaines Street
Tallahassee, FL 32301
904-488-1234

Georgia
Georgia Public Service Commission
162 State Office Building
244 Washington Street, SW
Atlanta, GA 30334
404-656-4501

Hawaii
Public Service Commission of the State of Hawaii
1164 Bishop Street, Suite 911
Honolulu, HI 96813
808-548-3990

Idaho
Idaho Public Utilities Commission
Statehouse
Boise, ID 83720
208-334-3143

Illinois
Illinois Commerce Commission
525 East Capitol Avenue
Springfield, IL 62706
217-782-7295

Indiana
Indiana Public Service Commission
901 State Office Building
Indianapolis, IN 46204
317-232-2701

Iowa
Iowa State Commerce Commission
Lucas Building
Des Moines, IA 50319
515-281-5979

Kansas
Kansas State Corporation Commission
State Office Building
Topeka, KS 66612
913-296-3326

Kentucky
Kentucky Public Service Commission
730 Schenkel Lane
Frankfort, KY 40602
502-564-3940

Louisiana
State of Louisiana Public Service Commission
One American Place, Suite 1630
Baton Rouge, LA 70825
504-342-4427

Maine
Maine Public Utilities Commission
242 State Street
Augusta, ME 04333
207-289-3831

Maryland
Maryland Public Service Commission
231 East Baltimore Street
Baltimore, MD 21202
301-659-6000

Massachusetts
Massachusetts Department of Public Utilities
100 Cambridge Street
Boston, MA 02202
617-727-3500

Michigan
Michigan Public Service Commission
6545 Mercantile Way
Lansing, MI 48909
517-373-3244

Minnesota
Minnesota Public Service Commission
780 American Center Building
160 East Kellogg Blvd.
St. Paul, MN 55155
612-296-7124

Mississippi
Mississippi Public Service Commission
19th Floor, Walter Sillers State Office Building
Jackson, MS 39205
601-961-5400

Missouri
Missouri Public Service Commission
Truman State Office Building
Jefferson City, MO 65102
314-751-7494

Montana
Montana Public Service Commission
2701 Prospect Avenue
Helena, MT 59620
406-444-6177

Nebraska
Nebraska Public Service Commission
301 Centennial Mall South
Lincoln, NE 68509
402-471-3101

Nevada
Public Service Commission of Nevada
505 East King Street
Carson City, NV 89710
702-885-4180

New Hampshire
New Hampshire Utilities Commission
8 Old Suncook Road
Concord, NH 03301
603-271-2431

New Jersey
New Jersey Board of Public Utilities
1100 Raymond Blvd.
Newark, NJ 07102
201-648-2026

New Mexico
New Mexico State Corporation Commission
Bataan Memorial Building
Santa Fe, NM 87503
505-827-3361

New York
New York Public Service Commission
Empire State Plaza
Albany, NY 12223
518-474-7080

North Carolina
North Carolina Utilities Commission
430 North Salisbury Street
Raleigh, NC 27602
919-733-4249

North Dakota
North Dakota Public Service Commission
State Capitol
Bismarck, ND 58505
701-224-2400

Ohio
Ohio Public Utilities Commission
180 East Broad Street
Columbus, OH 43215
614-466-3016

Oklahoma
Oklahoma Corporation Commission
Jim Thorpe Office Building
Oklahoma City, OK 73105
405-521-2307

Oregon
Public Utility Commissioner
300 Labor & Industries Building
Salem, OR 97310
503-378-4620

Pennsylvania
Pennsylvania Public Utility Commission
P.O. Box 3265
Harrisburg, PA 17120
717-783-1740

Rhode Island
Rhode Island Public Utilities Commission
100 Orange Street
Providence, RI 02903
401-277-3500

South Carolina
South Carolina Public Service Commission
111 Doctors Circle
Columbus, SC 29211
803-758-3621

South Dakota
South Dakota Public Utilities Commission
Capitol Building
Pierre, SD 57501
605-773-3201

Tennessee
Tennessee Public Service Commission
C1-120 Cordell Hull Building
Nashville, TN 37219
615-741-2904

Texas
Public Utility Commission of Texas
7800 Shoal Creek Blvd.
Suite 400-N
Austin, TX 78757
512-458-0100

Utah
Public Service Commission of Utah
160 East 300 South
Salt Lake City, UT 84145
801-530-6713

Vermont
Vermont Public Service Board
120 State Street
Montpelier, VT 05602
802-828-2358

Virginia
Virginia State Corporation Commission
P.O. Box 1197
Richmond, VA 23209
804-786-3672

Washington
Washington Utilities and Transportation Commission
Highways-License Building
Olympia, WA 98504
206-753-6423

West Virginia
West Virginia Public Service Commission
201 Brooks Street
Charleston, WV 25323
304-340-0300

Wisconsin
Wisconsin Public Service Commission
477 Hill Farms State Office Building
Madison, WI 53707
608-266-1241

Wyoming
Wyoming Public Service Commission
Capitol Hill Building
320 West 25th Street
Cheyenne, WY 82002
307-777-7427

INDEX

Numbers followed by "t" denote tables; those in *italics* denote figures.